YOU'VE

ALWAYS

BEEN

WRONG

YOU'VE ALWAYS BEEN WRONG

RENÉ DAUMAL

Tu t'es toujours trompé

Introduction by Jack Daumal

Translated by Thomas Vosteen

University of Nebraska Press

Lincoln and London

1995

Photographs of René Daumal on pages i, iii, v, vii, ix, and 7 taken by Rose Adler, 1928. Courtesy Colette Weil. © 1995 by the University of Nebraska Press. Originally published as *Tu t'es toujours trompé* © copyright Éditions Mercure de France 1970. All rights reserved. Manufactured in the United States of America. ⊗ The paper in this book meets the minimum requirements of American National Standard for Information Sciences – Permanence of Paper for Printed Library Materials, ANSI Z39.48-1984. The text is set in Matthew Carter's Galliard types. Typeset by Keystone. Book design by R. Eckersley. Library of Congress Cataloging-in-Publication Data Daumal, René, 1908–1944.
[Tu t'es toujours trompé. English]
You've always been wrong / René Daumal ; introduction by Jack Daumal ; translated by Thomas Vosteen.
p. cm. – (French modernist library.)
Original title on t.p.: Tu t'es toujours trompé.
Includes bibliographical references and index.
ISBN 0-8032-1699-8 (alk. paper) I. Title.
II. Series. PQ2607.A86T813
1995 844'.912–dc20
94-37337
CIP

CONTENTS

Daumal: Life and Works

René Daumal's life and work belong to two seemingly antipodal currents: one is loosely termed avant-garde in that it challenges cultural sclerosis, and the other can be qualified as traditionalist insofar as it is a quest for lasting values.

Like his literary ancestor, Arthur Rimbaud, Daumal was born in the Ardennes region of northern France and lived a short but intense life (1908–44) devoted to challenging passively accepted ideas concerning the nature of reality. Obsessed even in early childhood by the finality of death, he performed adolescent 'experiments' which consisted in inhaling carbon tetrachloride fumes to see what happens as consciousness turns away from its normal sensory orientation to the world. He did this hundreds of times; no wonder, then, that he died, lungs weakened, of tuberculosis at age thirty-six.

He was not alone in his rebellion. Inspired in spirit and in spelling by Alfred Jarry, the inventor of Pataphysics,[1] he and his companions at the *lycée* in Reims called themselves Les Phrères Simplistes (The Simplist[ic] Brothers) and engaged in metaphysical experimentation with and without chemical stimulation to the brain. Another of the Phrères, Roger Gilbert-Lecomte, was tormented less by the specter of death than by regret at having been born at all; he was to die a heroin addict just a few months before Daumal, also at the age of thirty-six. By the end of the 1920s when they were arriving in Paris, the 'communion' that the Phrères had already experienced together provided the ideological basis for their short-lived review (1928–30) whose title, *Le Grand Jeu* (*The Great Game*), also became the name of their group. Only three numbers were published; a fourth, planned for autumn 1932, never saw the light of day.

It was during this period of vitality for the *Grand Jeu* that Daumal composed a series of thematically related essays which would appear after his death grouped under the title *Tu t'es toujours trompé* (*You've Always Been Wrong*). In its style and content, the work is a clear statement of Daumal's political and, especially, philosophical concerns at the time of its composition; it is also a clear presage of the esoteric or metaphysical course his writing and thinking would take in his later poetry and essays and in the two works for which he is today best known: *La Grande Beuverie* (*A Night of Serious Drinking*), which is a parody of cultural institutions, and *Le Mont Analogue* (*Mount Analogue*), an allegory of the metaphysical quest. In its call for awakening, *You've Always Been Wrong* still speaks to that part of us which, discontent with this or that aspect of the status quo, realizes that change starts first within oneself.

Starting from a childhood obsession with the void, Daumal's thought was nourished early on by voracious reading which, aside from the classics of French culture, included significantly a wide variety of works on occultism. Often with his Phrères Simplistes comrades, he attempted various experiments, aside from the dangerous inhalations of carbon tetrachloride: extra-retinal vision, astral projection, telepathy, lucid dreaming, and so on.

Simultaneously, he was a remarkably bright student, finishing his *baccalauréat* at the age of seventeen. Shortly thereafter, he entered the Lycée Henri-IV in Paris in order to prepare for the qualifying examinations for entrance into the Ecole Normale Supérieure. His teacher at Henri-IV was the famous writer-philosopher Alain – the pseudonym of Emile Chartier – whose distaste for formal philosophical discourse and preference for more literary (jargon-free) forms of expression may well have had a determining influence. Due to a temporary bout of amnesia caused by a fall in his garden on 8 June 1927, Daumal did not pass the entrance examination, and therefore enrolled at the Sorbonne in October of the same year, subsequently earning a *certificat* in Psychology (2 July 1928) and another in Ethics and Sociology (29 June 1929). Finally, at the end of June 1931, he finished his *licence* in philosophy with two *certificats* in the General History of Philosophy and General Philosophy and Logic. He did all of this while remaining involved with the *Grand Jeu* and learning Sanskrit on his own.

It was also during this period (around the beginning of 1930, as he was finishing *You've Always Been Wrong*) that he began his relation-

ship with Alexandre de Salzmann, who introduced him to the esoteric teachings of George Ivanovich Gurdjieff. Just because he possessed a mind capable of intellectual rigor, whether in literature, philosophy, or the sciences (he would work starting in 1936 as a science
editor for the *Encyclopédie Française*) doesn't mean he dropped his
interest in the more esoteric aspects of metaphysics. On the contrary,
he wanted above all to impart scientific rigor to his search, to put
forth his inner experiences as 'proof' (as they indeed were, to him)
of the existence of an entire realm of experience not considered as
conventional within Western culture and philosophy. The *Grand Jeu*
group had served the barely postadolescent Daumal as a moral support; after its collapse, he continued his quest on his own, deriv-
ing emotional, mental, and spiritual support from Véra Milanova
(whom he married in February 1931), from the Gurdjieff group,
and from various literary figures of the time who recognized his ge-
nius as a thinker and his warmth as a friend; one such friend and
associate was Jean Paulhan of the *Nouvelle Revue Française*, to which
Daumal contributed various short articles on contemporary culture
observed from the viewpoint of Pataphysics (titled 'La Pataphysique
du mois' – 'This Month's Pataphysics'). His various occupations
over his short life – for example, accompanying the Indian dancer
Uday Shankar on a tour of the United States (7 December 1932 to 3
April 1933), editing the *Encyclopédie Française*, a very brief stint in the
army (from 19 April to 26 July 1933, when he was discharged because of poor health), various translations from English (most nota-
bly Hemingway's *Death in the Afternoon* and D. T. Suzuki's *Essays in
Zen Buddhism*) – were, in financial terms, little more than means to
fend off starvation. No matter what his transient occupations were at
any given time, however, the greater part of his energy and attention
remained focused throughout his life on his quest for gnosis – direct,
experiential knowledge of a reality qualified by the dominant culture
as metaphysical.

And that is precisely the crux of the problematic one encounters
on any approach to René Daumal, be it Daumal the individual or the
texts produced by Daumal the writer. He was acutely aware of the
limits of his language, one based in the dualism of Western culture

which defines metaphysics as that which is beyond lived experience and 'impossible to relate' verbally, as Daumal put it in his second essay on his asphyxiation experiments.[2] The contradiction must have been hard to bear: on one hand, Daumal considered it his dharma,[3] his life's calling, to be a writer (more specifically, a poet); on the other, his central concern – his obsession – was something which Western dualism posits as unreal, inexistent, and therefore silent, yet something which he insisted that every particle of his body and mind had directly experienced.

It therefore comes as no surprise that nondualism stands out as a major theme in *You've Always Been Wrong*. An isolated subject striving for individual(istic) self-expression is scarcely in a position to give textual reality to a transpersonal experience which Daumal would describe later (1936) as 'eternal' in his essay 'Clavicules d'un grand jeu poétique.'[4] What arises from this unmediated experience, if indeed a poet has been able to infuse it into his text, is the sense of an 'eternal return,' an obsessive, anxiety-producing feeling of *déjà vu* ('paramnesia') which must be 'overcome' by both poet and reader through what Daumal cryptically terms 'a contact made by consciousness with the universal' which transforms the 'already seen' (*déjà vu*) into the 'eternally seen.' The poet suggests the universal of consciousness through the particular of a given text; the reader willing to perform the requisite 'contact' with consciousness can use the text as a window into the feeling of 'something that has been in existence for all eternity.'

By espousing the Hindu concept of Advaita (nondualism) in *You've Always Been Wrong*, Daumal seems to be making a case for a kind of deconstruction, albeit one which is somewhat at variance with that of Jacques Derrida. As David Loy observes,

From the non-dualist perspective, the problem with Derrida's radical critique of Western philosophy is that it is not radical enough: his deconstruction is incomplete because it does not deconstruct itself and attain that *clôture* which . . . is the opening to something else. This is why Derrida remains in the halfway-house of proliferating 'pure textuality,' whereas deconstruction could lead to a transformed mode of experiencing the world.[5]

It is precisely the type of ludic 'bad infinity' produced by this 'pro-liferating "pure textuality"' and often dramatized in (post)modern-ist texts (the examples of Franz Kafka and Maurice Blanchot come easily to mind) that Daumal's conscious, willed, deconstructive 'contact' avoids. The exoteric surfaces of Daumal's texts are surpris-ingly 'readerly,' given their hermetic underpinnings and their esoteric depth. Next to the 'writerly' quality which stands as a barrier to those readers unwilling to participate in the (co)production of a (post)-modern text's meaning, such texts as *A Night of Serious Drinking* and *Mount Analogue* stand as paragons of (apparent) transparency. Yet the initiated reader, the one who is willing to make the 'contact' pre-scribed by Daumal, will in the end approach Daumal's texts in a 'writerly' way by piercing their limpid surfaces beneath which lies not just a communication, but the 'communion' which the Phrères Sim-plistes claimed to have during their *Grand Jeu* days. Indeed, as we read under 'Pataphysics' in *You've Always Been Wrong*, the same (pa-taphysical) operation should be performed on our perception of the world: 'To know X = to know (Everything − X).' What is left once X is subtracted from everything is a void with the shape of X, X without its name: a direct, unmediated experience of X.

Daumal, the Grand Jeu, and Surrealism

In its aims and methods, the *Grand Jeu* was in many ways similar to the Surrealist group; but it was different enough to arouse André Breton's hostility. The *Grand Jeu* thus found itself embroiled in 1929 in a quasi-political standoff which culminated in an event now seen as pivotal in the history of Surrealism. Since *You've Always Been Wrong* was composed between 1928 and 1930, it may be of some interest to a present-day reader of this text, the most politically ori-ented of all of Daumal's writings, to delve into a few of the event's more pertinent details.

In February 1929, Breton sent out a letter polling the leading avant-garde intellectuals of the day, including Daumal and his *Grand Jeu* comrades Roger Gilbert-Lecomte and Roger Vailland, on the question of the desirability of collective as opposed to purely individ-ual revolutionary action. It was a loaded question: in 1926, Antonin

Artaud and Philippe Soupault had already incurred Breton's wrath for their deviations from collective orthodoxy; a forced exclusion from the group had rewarded and confirmed their individualism. Those who answered the 1929 poll (again including the *Grand Jeu* protagonists) were then sent a letter convening them to a meeting on 11 March at the bar du Château. The ostensible purpose of the meeting, as announced in the letter, was to discuss the fate of Leon Trotsky, who had been ousted from the Communist Party on 14 November 1927, deported to Alma-Ata on 17 January 1928, and expelled from the Soviet Union in January 1929. The events of the meeting showed up the announced agenda for the pretext it in fact was. Breton immediately declared that the Trotsky question could not be considered until the air was cleared concerning certain less-than-militant attitudes observed among fellow revolutionaries. And a trial of the *Grand Jeu* commenced.

There were a number of grievances brought forth against the defendants. Two of them are particularly helpful for the purpose of distinguishing Daumal from Breton:[6] the first number of *Le Grand Jeu* repeatedly used the word 'God,' at one point clearly identified as God in three persons; members of the *Grand Jeu* had participated in the activities of the théâtre Alfred-Jarry. Although no specific answers to these objections were reported, each one in its way raises the issue which perhaps most clearly demarcates the politics of Surrealism from that of (Daumal and) the *Grand Jeu*. While leftward-leaning, the *Grand Jeu*, by the very fact that it saw any declaration – political, philosophical, or otherwise – as immediately placing limits on the absolute truth, and eschewing any permanently defined position, was in fact more anarchical than political in that it challenged all political order, left or right, on a permanent basis. From this basis, we can supply hypothetical answers to Breton's grievances:

(1) The use of the word 'God,' also one of the central issues of *You've Always Been Wrong*, was more a gesture of defiance against rigid ideology than a bow to tradition. Perhaps as an indirect reply to Breton's challenge, Daumal and Gilbert-Lecomte, in a cosigned article which appeared in the spring of 1929 in *Le Grand Jeu* (no.2),

declared in a footnote to the lead essay, 'Mise au point ou Casse-dogme' ('Clarification, or Dogmaclasm'):

Since we have at times designated absolute reality by the word 'God' and do not want to deprive ourselves of a word simply because such shabby use has been made of it, let's be perfectly clear:

God is that limit-state of any consciousness which is Con-sciousness grasping itself without the help of any individuality or, if you wish, without the support of any particular object.[7]

(2) As Alfred Jarry had already clearly demonstrated, truth is pata-physical and absurd. Participating in a theater bearing his name is at very least an homage to the *Grand Jeu*'s spiritual forebear. It is perhaps also a way to demonstrate solidarity with Antonin Artaud, cofounder with Roger Vitrac of the théâtre Alfred-Jarry. In 1926, Artaud and the Surrealists mutually parted company, with the Sur-realists claiming that Artaud's individualistic interest in literature was incompatible with the collective thrust toward 'Revolution,' which he saw mainly as an inner spiritual phenomenon; indeed, it was Artaud's opinion that the Surrealists, rather than following their original mission of challenging the consensus upon which reality is commonly experienced, had become much too interested in matter for its own sake. Similarly, Daumal would later (1932) state in a brief essay intended for the unpublished fourth number of *Le Grand Jeu* that the Surrealists 'too often fall back into the old materialism ("primacy of matter over thought") which is never anything more than a one-legged dualism (just as the old idealism, which omits matter, is a one-legged dualism).'[8] The trial of the bar du Château was scarcely the last salvo fired in an ongoing conflict which resem-bled more a lovers' quarrel than an outright war. In the 1930 *Second Manifesto of Surrealism*, Breton would express his admiration for a poem by Daumal, 'Feux à volonté' ('Fires at Will'), published in the 1929 second number of *Le Grand Jeu*, adding that such a talent surely had no reason not to join the Surrealist camp. Daumal's reply, pub-lished in the autumn of 1930 in *Le Grand Jeu* (no.3), under the title 'Open Letter to André Breton Concerning Relations between Sur-

realism and the *Grand Jeu*,[9] while insisting on the differences of method and philosophy which separate and distinguish the two groups, expresses admiration for Breton and a cautious solidarity[10] with the Surrealist goal known commonly as 'le point suprême,' the point at which, as Daumal somewhat tauntingly proposes, the Surrealists can some day meet the *Grand Jeu*. Therein lies the crux of the difference. For Surrealism, the 'supreme point,' a matter of belief,[11] is perpetually deferred to a virtual horizon. For Daumal and the *Grand Jeu*, it is simultaneously virtual and eternally present, accessible here and now through a voluntary act of consciousness. It is this act, that of awakening, that is the central motif of *You've Always Been Wrong*.

In the same 'Open Letter to André Breton,' Daumal also expressed the wish that the *Grand Jeu* would go down in the 'history of cataclysms.' Time would demonstrate that it is difficult if not impossible to persuade the collectivity to undergo a cataclysm *willingly*. On the individual and ethical level, one can come to an awareness of the ego's relativity and lack of a consistent center. The experience can be *de*scribed, but to *pre*scribe it is a political gesture which runs the risk of going beyond liberation into chaos. Near the end of his life, Daumal wrote a poem that is arguably his greatest: 'The Holy War.' The 'war' in question is to be waged on a personal level against all obstacles blocking the full awakening of an individual's consciousness. He starts the poem by denying that it is a 'true poem,' even though its subject is a 'real war,' because if a 'real poet' were to speak, 'there would be a great silence . . . the silence of a thousand thunderclaps.'

It is this same silence that *You've Always Been Wrong* can make audible by providing the requisite initiation to Daumal's poetic practice through his theoretical prose.

The Edition

This translation of a series of Daumal's youthful essays, grouped as a whole under the title *You've Always Been Wrong*, is in fact the edition of an edition. Written between 1928 and 1930, the essays were first published as a whole work by Mercure de France in 1970 under the title *Tu t'es toujours trompé*. The edition was the work of Jack Daumal, a professor at the University of Cairo, who assembled various of his brother René's manuscripts, parts of which had been previously published elsewhere, and added his own introduction and annotations and a long final section bearing the title 'Documents.' This latter portion of the book consists of five parts: (1) a history of the *Grand Jeu* (titled 'The Death of the *Grand Jeu*') told through a series of letters written by or sent to René, a portion of an article René published in the review *Europe* in 1936, and a passage from *Mount Analogue*, all commented on by Jack; (2) three drafts of an outline, written by René, of *You've Always Been Wrong*; (3) 'Diverse Notes on Pataphysics,' by René; (4) another series of René's letters, with commentary by Jack, recounting the difficulties which prevented the 'Poem to God and Man' from being published until this edition; (5) 'The Disarray of Young French Intellectuals in 1925,' an article by Benjamin Crémieux.

From this latter section, I have retained for this translation items 2 and 3 *in toto*: the three drafts of an outline of *You've Always Been Wrong* give some idea of the genesis of Daumal's thought and can perhaps serve as a guide to the work's motifs; the 'Diverse Notes on Pataphysics' are, in my opinion, a good illustration of their subject. I also retained a smaller portion of the *Europe* article, 'Sur le scientisme et la révolution' ('On Scientism and the Revolution'), which was in fact a review of a book by Jean Fiolle, *Scientisme et science*, published by Mercure de France in 1936. In its last few paragraphs, Daumal clearly and succinctly situates himself on the left end of the political spectrum.[12] I felt this was necessary in order to counter any eventual suspicion that his penchant for metaphysics and its concomitant traditionalism might induce him to lean toward the fascist right. If it can be said that Daumal abandoned the cause of the Revolution during the last half of his short life, it is because, as he followed the Gurdjieff teachings, he became introspective, hence apolitical, and, in the long run, physically weakened.

Although I have not included a translation of the letters documenting the vagaries of the 'Poem to God and Man,' I have summarized their contents in a note to the poem. On the other hand, I felt it superfluous to include the details relative to the 'Death of the *Grand Jeu*,' or the article by Crémieux, which I feel are unnecessary for the full appreciation of the text's immediate impact on today's reader. Specialists wishing to do further research into this historical period can easily consult the original Mercure de France volume.

The rest of the original Jack Daumal edition has been retained and translated in its entirety, including the introduction and all liminal notes and annotations.[13] My editorial role has involved providing this translator's introduction, an index, and a number of translator's footnotes to clarify certain of Daumal's more obscure allusions and references. Because René Daumal accompanied his text with footnotes and Jack Daumal also added commentary in the form of footnotes, the reader will find three types of annotation presented, with each note followed by either RD (René Daumal), JD (Jack Daumal), or TV (Thomas Vosteen; i.e., translator's note) to indicate its author.

Style and Tone

It is of course the reader's prerogative to declare how the text sounds.

My effort as translator has been to render a text whose author wants to speak directly to his reader, without typographical mediation. As I read the original text, I hear a rather precocious twenty-year-old student of philosophy trying to escape the formal style by which he has undergone his (academic) philosophical training; whence the preference I have given to elisions such as 'you've,' designed to convey the familiarity of the French 'tu' by which a projected interlocutor is addressed. In the same movement, one of passionate involvement with the ideas expressed, the tone gives way to the formal, that of a lecture passionately delivered to a vast imagined audience, a crowd of familiars eager to hear . . . A question comes forth, and authorial consciousness snaps back to familiarity.

My strongest hope is that this is a pataphysical translation, as Pataphysics is the 'science of the particular.'[14]

Lexical Challenges

Those who know French will immediately recognize the problems involved in translating certain French words into English. I list the following words because, aside from being problematic even to the point of cliché, they are central to Daumal's repertory:

esprit: 'Spirit' or 'mind'? I have done my honest best to render this word precisely according to its contextual resonance. Although Daumal is clearly interested in 'spiritual' questions, the mind as cognitive antenna of spirit plays a paramount role for individual consciousness as it is directly involved in the experience of reality.

évidence: The most accurate rendering of this word is the clumsy 'obviousness,' that which is irreducible as an immediate element of consciousness. I have preferred the word 'clarity,' although 'evidence' has at times seemed appropriate. One possible translation of the title of the Gallimard edition of Daumal's essays, *L'Evidence Absurde*, is 'meaningless clarity.'

ascèse: Although 'ascesis' (or 'askesis') does exist in English, I have preferred 'self-denial' or 'abnegation' to convey a sense of withdrawal from the world and purgation of the self.

expérience / expérimental: One of the *Grand Jeu*'s (and thus, Daumal's) major goals was to develop an 'experimental metaphysics,' that is, a metaphysics based on empirical findings and repeatable experimentation rather than abstract speculation. The enterprise hinged, however, on a personal (i.e., subjective) experience such as the one Daumal performed with the aid of carbon tetrachloride. In English we must decide whether sense data we undergo or seek out are simply an 'experience' or in fact an 'experiment.' In French, 'expérience' is adequate to both situations; and 'expérimental' can signify both 'experimental' and 'experiential.' One can strongly speculate that Daumal well enjoyed and exploited the ambiguity which indeed inheres in the French term.

conscience: Although Daumal is clearly aware of its moral dimension, 'consciousness' is, for him, first immediate 'awareness' and then, through reflection, a matter of 'conscience,' morals and (personal) conduct.

homme: 'Man'; Daumal footnotes the word 'hommes' in his 1935 pataphysical essay 'Têtes fatiguées' ('Weary Heads') as follows: 'To avoid circumlocution, I ask once and for all that this word be understood as including "and women."'[15]

Daumal in English

Ground was first broken when Roger Shattuck published his translation of *Le Mont Analogue* in 1959. Since then, a number of other works of fiction and nonfiction (a distinction one might well consider specious as regards Daumal) have appeared at varying intervals. I hope that this translation of *Tu t'es toujours trompé* can shed more light on its predecessors.

The following list of major translations into English of Daumal's texts published as single volumes gives the most recent known edition and is arranged alphabetically by name of translator. The original French Daumal titles are those in which the material translated in the preceding volume in English can be found. All of the French editions of Daumal's writings that are cited here are published by Gallimard:

Coward, David, and E. A. Lovatt. *A Night of Serious Drinking*. Boston: Shambhala, 1979. (*La Grande Beuverie*, 1938.)

Knight, Kelton W. *Le Contre-Ciel*. New York: Peter Lang, 1990. (*Le Contre-ciel*, 1970.)

Levi, Louise Landes. *Rasa, or Knowledge of the Self. Essays on Indian Aesthetics and Selected Sanskrit Studies*. New York: New Directions, 1982. (*Bharata*, 1970; *Le Contre-ciel*, 1970; *L'Evidence Absurde*, 1972; *Les Pouvoirs de la Parole*, 1972.)

Polizzotti, Mark. *The Powers of the Word. Selected Essays and Notes, 1927–1943*. San Francisco: City Lights, 1991. (*L'Evidence Absurde*, 1972; *Les Pouvoirs de la Parole*, 1972.)

Powrie, Phil. *The Lie of the Truth*. Madras: Hanuman, 1989. ('Le Mensonge de la vérité,' in *Les Pouvoirs de la Parole*, 1972.)

Shattuck, Roger. *A Fundamental Experiment*. Madras: Hanuman, 1987. ('Une Expérience fondamentale,' in *Chaque fois que l'aube paraît*, 1953, republished as 'Le Souvenir déterminant' in *Les Pouvoirs de la Parole*, 1972.)

Shattuck, Roger. *Mount Analogue. A Novel of Symbolically Authentic Non-Euclidean Adventures in Mountain Climbing*. Boston: Shambhala, 1986. (*Le Mont Analogue*, 1952.)

Further bibliographical information concerning Daumal and Gilbert-Lecomte can be found in

Powrie, Phil. *René Daumal and Roger Gilbert-Lecomte: a Bibliography*. London: Grant and Cutler, 1988.

Sigoda, Pascal. *René Daumal, Dossiers*. Paris: L'Age d'Homme, 1993.

INTRODUCTION
Jack Daumal

Until the last few years, literary professionals had respected one of the primary intentions of the *Grand Jeu* group: the refusal to 'participate,' to fit in to the literary and artistic movement of its time. Then, the inevitable happened.

Claudio Rugafiori's handsome book, *Il Grand Jeu* (Milan, 1967), the extraordinary Sima[2] expositions in Prague and then in Paris toward the end of 1968, and finally the publication of an important special issue of *Les Cahiers de l'Herne*[3] are such that henceforth the *Grand Jeu*, concurrently with surrealism, will no doubt mark one of the prime moments in the literary and artistic history of the period between the First and the Second World Wars.

Therefore, if we now publish texts by René Daumal dating from 1928 to 1930, no new harm is done; the *Grand Jeu* period has already become fodder for the type of scholarly, biographical, historical, psychologistic criticisms which have been wreaking havoc in many areas for quite some time; it's a well-known fact that the calling and ability of worms is to gnaw and digest corpses, only corpses.

But there were still other serious reasons for not publishing these texts. In 1930, René Daumal had found the person and the thing which changed his life and gave order to his existence.[4] From then on, he was always very cautious about letting anyone see, read, or reedit anything he might have written before that encounter. He explained his own reasons very well in 1936, in his preface to *Le Contre-Ciel*:[5]

> I hesitated before publishing this collection. I know that you don't learn to swim instantly, that you must splash around just for fun to get the feel of it even before you find out that there are rivers to cross. But you don't have to make a show of your learning process. Nonetheless, a few people I respect assure me that

there are herein glimpses of real shores, that these writings no longer belong to me and that they can be useful for others. I yield, but I'm taking a few precautions.

The essay on poetic creation which opens this book was written about six years ago.[6] I have cut from it only a few factual errors. The rest of it, taken literally, is not without truth, but some of these truths have taken root in me only recently, and today I would express them in simpler terms. I would not even mention the others which have not come to maturity. Here, however, is this essay, as reckless as it may be. I was just beginning, as I wrote it, to rid myself of philosophical jargon and a certain facile pathos. But there were a few seeds of thought in it; and like chemical substances in the nascent state, they perhaps have particular virtues.

If one day I create a poem, people will understand my present reluctance to apply that word to describe the lyric pieces which follow . . .[7]

They are closer to a scream than a song. They were valves opening to let off pressure while waiting for something better. I've found something better to release most of the torments which those outpourings could not completely soothe. Better and simpler. Perhaps only one of these torments can not be reduced, because it doesn't come from without, and the traces of this torment, now still in the nascent state, are what can justify the publication of the others. Unlearning daydreaming, learning to think, unlearning philosophizing, learning to express: these things aren't done in a day. And yet we have so few days in which to do it.

I am again feeling these scruples, perhaps even more intensely. If we weren't in this dark age, I wouldn't hesitate: nothing of that which René Daumal rejected as being imperfect, insufficient, or dangerous would be published by my consent. But in these decades which the people of the West are now living through, for this fervent, painful, earnest, and so often wretched time of youth, Daumal and his friends of the *Grand Jeu* can be of some real interest. Perhaps some will see themselves echoed in a certain 'jargon,' in a 'certain facile pathos,' and will understand in the end how my brother could come forth into a fourteen-year period, 1930 to 1944: a time of achievement, of a direct ascent after going round and round in circles – a march toward victory after the long dark night traversed only by will-o'-the-wisps and fleeting glimmers.

Therefore, let us exhume, not a work, but a strange document, rich in memories for me – Roger Gilbert-Lecomte and the 'simplists,' the prestigious Dida de Mayo, the warm and generous Monny de Boully . . .[8] Memories of their passionate youthful discussions, of those noble souls marked by an intellectualistic teaching and attracted, fascinated by abstract ideologies, Bolshevism in particular.

A Note on the Manuscript

The manuscript of fifty-six pages, bearing no title, dates from 1926–28. In it, a youthful, uncompromising Marxism is trying to gain as an ally truths already perceived or glimpsed in the forest of the authentic Traditions[9] of the Orient and to safeguard a certain form of 'metaphysics.' . . .

But this manuscript is supplemented by typewritten copies of the first thirty-eight pages. These copies furnish us with new material of varying degrees of importance: corrections and revisions bear witness to reconsiderations subsequent to the *Grand Jeu* period – interventions which followed the decisive encounter with the Teaching[10] to which Alexandre de Salzmann introduced him. Across the first page of one of these typewritten copies, and placed as a title, or rather an epigraph, are the following words:

UNFINISHED because of
DEATH

I would swear it is written in my brother's hand.

Of course, we have retained the definitive, typewritten, revised, and corrected text for the first thirty-eight pages. Starting on page thirty-nine of the manuscript, marginal comments (often ironic and caustic) in the author's handwriting suggest that René Daumal intended to pursue his corrections and revisions of the original manuscript; they will be annotated in the text at the points which correspond to their original occurrence.   JD

AN APPEAL TO CONSCIOUSNESS

Spiritual Death

You've always been wrong. Like me, like any man, you've let yourself slide down easy, futile slopes. Your mind has traveled only in dreams toward the truth. Compare your thought today with the things which stand in your way; your fondest theories vanish before the wall of appearances. That veil of colored shapes, sounds, and other perceptible qualities that is so easily termed illusory is solid, nevertheless. This is where you started, but you chose the wrong door. Or rather you thought you started; you fell asleep on the threshold and dreamed your beliefs about the world and the mind.

Today I'm waiting for you on the threshold. We'll take our first halting steps together. I'm asking you first to look around you, right now, with total candor. See what is before you. Above all, don't start to question the reality of this world. By what authority could you judge it? Do you know what absolute reality is? Whoever starts on a voyage must start from wherever he is; he mustn't think the destination is already reached just because he has an accurate and detailed itinerary in his hands; the line he has drawn on a map has no meaning unless he can pinpoint his present location. You as well: look at yourself. I mean: wake up, find yourself. The place *where you are* is where you have to begin: the present state of your consciousness, together with all that it contains. And all our speculation will never amount to more than the itinerary of a merely possible voyage.

Any metaphysics that is sufficient unto itself suggests the vain pleasure of a man who whiles away the hours reading travel guides and timetables, tracing out routes on a map, and thinks that he is actually traveling. Up to now, philosophers seem to have done little more than this; or, if some of them have actually traveled, none has managed to make the fact show through. And so all philosophy, even if it were once experienced by its creator as real, remains a sterile and useless game for mankind.

. . .

What I would like you to try to do with me can be summed up in two words: *remain awake*. I first asked you to awaken, to realize what you're conscious of right now. You are conscious of a continual change. You moreover felt, in one way or another, a need to become something that you are not yet. But maybe you state, because you've misunderstood me, that you feel nothing of the sort. Even then you can realize that if you passively accept the conditions imposed on your consciousness, you're asleep. Awakening is not a state, it's an act. And people are much less often awake than their words would have us believe.

A man wakes up in the morning in bed. Scarcely on his feet, he's already asleep again. Going through all the automatic impulses which make his body get dressed, go out, walk, get to work, go through the prescribed daily routine, eat, chat, read a newspaper (as it's generally the body which takes care of all that by itself) – doing all that – he's sleeping. In order to wake up, he'd have to think, 'All that agitation is outside of me.' He would need to perform an act of *reflection*. But if that act triggers in him new automatic impulses, those of memory or of reasoning, his voice can continue to claim that he's still reflecting: but he has fallen back asleep. He can thus spend entire days without waking for a single moment. Just think about this when you're in public and you'll see yourself surrounded by a crowd of sleepwalkers. Man does not spend a third of his life, as they say, but nearly all his life sleeping in this true slumber of the mind. And it's easy for slumber, which is the *inertia* of consciousness, to catch man in its traps; for man, being naturally and *almost* irremediably lazy, might indeed be willing to awaken. But since the effort is repugnant to him, he would like that effort once it is put forth to place him (and naively he thinks it is possible) in a permanent or at least lengthy waking state. Then wanting to *rest* while in his *awakening*, he falls asleep. Just as one cannot *will* oneself to sleep, since willing, in whatever form, is still an awakening, one can remain awakened only if one wills it at every moment.

And the only direct act which you can carry out is that of awakening, of becoming conscious of yourself. Look back on what you think you've done since the beginning of today: this is perhaps the first time you've really awakened. And it's only now that you're conscious of all you've done as a thoughtless automaton. In most cases people never awaken even enough to realize that they have slept.

Right now, go ahead and accept, if you wish, this sleepwalker's existence. You will be able to behave in life as an idler, a worker, a peasant, a merchant, a diplomat, an artist, a philosopher, without ever awakening any more than just enough, now and then, to enjoy or suffer from the way in which you sleep. It might even be more convenient, without changing anything in your appearance, not to awaken at all.

And as the reality of mind lies in its *activity*, the very idea of a 'thinking substance' being nothing unless that idea is thought in the here and now, this sleep – this absence of action, this privation of thought – is truly *spiritual death*.

. . .

But if you have chosen to *be*, you have set forth on a difficult path which endlessly climbs and demands an unflagging effort. You are awakening; and immediately you have to awaken again. You awaken from your awakening. Your first awakening appears as slumber to your second awakening. This reflexive forward progress perpetually impels consciousness to action. Unlike other men the majority of whom do no more than awaken, fall asleep, awaken, and fall asleep, going up one rung of consciousness only to climb right back down, never rising above that zigzagging line, you *find yourself*, launched as you are on an indefinite trajectory of ever-renewed awakenings. And as nothing has value except for a perceiving consciousness, your reflection on that perpetual awakening motion toward the highest possible consciousness will comprise the science of sciences. I call it METAPHYSICS. But just because it is the science of sciences is no reason to forget that it will never be anything more than an itinerary, broadly sketched out in advance, for the actual journey. If you forget this, if you think you have finished waking up because you have planned in advance the conditions of your perpetual awakening, then at that point you will fall back asleep, falling asleep in spiritual Death.

Truisms

No cognition – considered as potential knowledge – has any value apart from its relation to a possible act of consciousness. In the area of everyday experience, the idea I have of a pear, or of England, provides me with nothing more than an anticipation of what I can experience by seeing or grasping the pear, sniffing it, tasting it, or by traveling to England. An 'object' is the *law* by which certain sensations can come to me and be transformed within me one by one.

These truisms are what the mind in quest of the real always finds at the beginning. The moment in thinking which they express – the empirical idealism of philosophers – is inevitable: Berkeley and the others, satisfied, stop here and fall asleep.[1] But don't let go of this slender Ariadne's thread, your own consciousness: you must now hold as real the very act which realizes a virtual cognition. By seeking it, you will break through this primal moment of idealism which, put back in its place in the dialectical[2] development of thought, remains *true*.

Scientific knowledge itself sets up a general anticipatory framework for the active cognition of particular objects. The physicist does not experience, properly speaking, the law of falling bodies: he knows only that he can experience through cognition the fall of a particular body according to a general law. I say 'the physicist' meaning 'as a physicist'; for another may take the law itself as an object of knowledge. And if the physicist himself succeeds in knowing it no longer only as a general relation but rather as the expression of a universal reality, at that moment he is more than a physicist. He is a *metaphysician*; not just because he 'goes beyond the field of physics,' but in the fullest sense as well, provided that his science of science is real[3] in the same sense in which I spoke previously about Metaphysics. Indeed, let us hold firmly to this principle: the knowledge of a *reality* as such can only be an act of cognition, an immediate act; and the only immediately performed act is that of *awakening*. Since the law is a general anticipatory framework for relationships between phenomena, knowing how to advance from the framework to the apprehension of a universal reality implies establishing the rules and conditions according to which the scientist's thought can be actualized. The physicist who awakens to his science becomes a metaphysician.

The supreme science, which I name Metaphysics, will thus express the possibility of the perpetual awakening of consciousness. And since the first awakening brings to me the whole field of my present perceptions, Metaphysics must give me mastery over all the concrete contents of my consciousness; and I must continually confront my consciousness with those contents.

Metaphysics, taken in itself, alone and as if it were self-justifying, becomes the subtlest subterfuge by which slumber creeps up on us; for if it expresses the possibility of an increasingly higher consciousness, it is only the *possibility* which it expresses. The possible as such is nothing, and to be content with the possible is to sleep. Hence, Metaphysics, to the extent that it is practiced for its own sake outside of any concrete criteria, is open to all criticisms.

Indeed, if we take any scientific theory in itself, whichever it may be, it will always appear as debatable, as dismissible and even as arbitrary as any metaphysical doctrine. For example, it would be enough just to cast doubt on the basic premises of science. The logical linkage of component parts establishes no more than the possibility of truth. If there is widespread agreement over scientific theories, it is thanks to experimental proof. Metaphysical doctrines are no more, no less debatable in themselves than the theories of the sciences; the existence of an experimental method which could be applied to them would be enough to foster a shared agreement among minds over metaphysical truth. Now, Metaphysics, like the sciences, starts from the concrete. If it is then organized into a set of abstract and general postulates, it is because it expresses only virtual knowledge; and in so doing, it proceeds no differently from science. Scientific theories and metaphysical systems are built on the same foundations, that is, all the modifications which consciousness *undergoes*. So it is not at all obvious *a priori* that a metaphysical experiment is impossible.

If the points of departure and the raw materials of science and metaphysics are the same, it is true that the former is based on a particular, artificially isolated aspect of the concrete; whereas the latter starts from the totality of concrete reality as it subsists in consciousness. Science proceeds from given perceptions without questioning the act of consciousness which makes them appear; it thus does not call for man to awaken. The initial fact of Metaphysics, as I have presented it, is the first act of awakening, an inner realization.

Any metaphysical experiment will therefore consist in an act of consciousness, that is, in an effort repugnant in the highest degree to human laziness. And that is why it is preferred in general to regard such an experience as impossible.

Metaphysical speculation, in beginning to live a life of its own, has forgotten its origin in the immediate experience of consciousness. Because of this oblivion, the metaphysician can exempt himself from turning for understanding to this experience, that of awakening. And, at one and the same time, metaphysics finds itself deprived of any criteria of truth. It tends toward forming logically ordered systems of relationships between abstract notions whose origin is no longer known. Such systems are always, necessarily, debatable and refutable. Since the point of departure of any speculation of this sort is an abstract notion, it will always be possible to deny the legitimacy of taking it as an origin and to demonstrate that it is not a primary notion, whether it is called Being, the One, God, Substance, or any other principle given as absolute. No one sees that the ideal form of a metaphysical system is that of the vicious circle. The point of departure is of little importance. All of human knowledge, if considered as valid in and of itself, is a gigantic vicious circle; as long as it is closed, the circle can be described starting at any point you like.

We can hope to reach the highest level of certainty possible for the human mind if, instead of trying to construct a metaphysical doctrine, or to establish discursive relationships between abstract notions, we rather take as the object of our science the metaphysical fact as such. No critique, no refutation has ever prevented man from practicing metaphysics. There is a metaphysical need, a metaphysical function of thinking; a science based on it is possible. If we stop taking metaphysical notions as givens and start trying to establish their meanings and their values on the basis of their experimental roots, an agreement on metaphysics conceived in this light may be reached among all those people who will voluntarily choose to remain awakened.

PROVOCATIONS TO SELF-DENIAL

If now someone asks, 'Why this perpetual race toward awakening, why attempt to be always more conscious, why will oneself out of the human condition, what for?,' tell him to look within himself with a clear gaze. If the answer, '*for* such and such a reason,' which the 'Why?' elicits doesn't come to him immediately, at least he will clearly see, if he really looks, the *because*. He will necessarily want to deliver himself from the human state, because he will see that state as intolerable. He may well have understood that remaining awake is not a state in which it is enough simply to stake his claim once and for all; that there is no middle ground between consciousness, an effort sustained in each instant, and absolute sleep; and therefore, if he doesn't want to *lose himself*, he must go unrelentingly forward. That reason, however clearly he may understand it, will be no more apt than any other abstract truth to *make him want* to go forward. The best reasons in the world will not get man going if nothing pushes him, even if a bit roughly, into taking the first step.

The vision of the intolerable is reason enough to establish for human consciousness the necessity to be transformed. This race is at first a flight. So I must first of all try to describe it as such. Then only will I be able to speak of the end, of this transformation's final goal as it is represented in awareness for the purpose of guiding the pursuit. This will be the particular object of Metaphysics, itself the forerunner of Self-Denial. Metaphysics would be no more than a closed system of abstractions, something 'up in the air,' if it were not continually and continuously connected to its concrete roots and, from the outset, to the direct experience of the INTOLERABLE.

That experience, as thought, is the *Vision of the Absurd*; as felt, it is *Suffering*. And these are two orders of incitement to self-denial, injunctions addressed to man and saying, 'Rise up to an ever-renewed awakening or otherwise sleep in spiritual death.'

I will strive to relive that first moment of the search, the one we often have to come back to. I will allow modes of feeling and thinking which I have long since succeeded in overcoming to unfold in me. I will even accept the *tone* which the new beginning, ever necessary, of these first steps imposes on my thought and speech, first steps which I want to take with you again and again.

I will describe one by one the Absurd Evidence of the intuited self through the *Revelation of Laughter*; the Absurd Evidence of the perception of the world through *Pataphysics*; and Absurd Evidence in human behavior as a principle of *Revolt*.

Then it will be possible for me to advance the Vision of the Absurd as an example of the first type of metaphysical experience.

The Revelation of Laughter

There will be the revelation of laughter for every man, but there will be nothing joyful about it. In my state of affairs, the world's sheaths turn inside out like the fingers of a glove: the obvious becomes absurd, light is a black veil, and a dazzling sun slumbers opposite my eyes.

For everyone there will be the revelation that any form is absurd once taken seriously. I hear in all human gullets a vocal mechanism speaking, rising up since adolescence; I hear it saying, in loutish muted echoes, clamoring or whispering in all modes of discourse: 'I am a man!' Whether he addresses another, himself, or the deafness of space, his speech implies an unquestioned and therefore unconscious affirmation: 'I am a man!' He concentrates all his energy on the task of propping up the monument, the Monumental Monument of human Dignity which justifies his slightest acts, his most secret thoughts, his heart's most intimate throbs. 'It is a man's role,' says the Human Man, 'to be a Man and to act, to think, and to feel as do I, a Man like Me.' At every moment, tremendous forces are being expended in him, working ever more to assure him of an affirmation which I can easily conceive as completely arbitrary. As I witness this spectacle, my breathing cracks and shakes me from head to toe. 'I am a man.' Why not say, 'I am Mister So-and-So,' or 'I am a merchant,' or 'French,' or 'the head of a household,' or 'a mammal,' or 'a philosopher,' or 'a rational animal'? Yet they say it! And it's all columns, capitals, pediments, turrets, watchtowers, fireworks, and weather vanes on the Monumental Monument of their Dignity. And it all adorns and upholds the Actions, the Thoughts, and the Feelings of these men, shadows of men self-assured straight to the death-marrow of their bones rotting in pride. HA! What a LAUGH!

Here's one getting on the bus. Nothing's on his mind, and as you can well imagine, he's not questioning his own existence any more than the reality or the dignity of the act he's performing. You might just as well say that this event is the center of his being, that it is his very being; or rather it's the shape of his nonbeing, the *hole* he's making in reality. I'm sure most men perform their favorite or habitual acts with the same degree of seriousness and conviction. This one, right now, is eternally getting on the bus. But, of course, he's not thinking about it since he's asleep. And as long as he doesn't wake up, each of his seeming acts, whatever they may appear to be, will always be nothing more than a way of not being. Making Art for Art's sake is just another bus ride. Here's a gent who holds truth as an ideal just as simply as the other one takes the bus. And this charitable old lady who's just put her contribution in the poor box: she's just as dead as the others. If we agree that the symbol *zero* can signify *not-being*, all these sleepwalkers differ one from the other as much as do the factors *0* x *3*, *0* x *8*, *0* x *17*, and so forth. There are an infinite number of ways of not being.

'I am a man.' They say it without amazement . . . And Laughter tortures me still before the spectacle of human actions.

. . .

What one takes absolutely seriously, what one doubts in no way whatsoever can take on the name *god*. Anything can be taken seriously. If I adopt the attitude of the gentleman who doesn't laugh and I gaze upon the infinite detail of forms, everything is god, each point in space, each instant of duration, each moment of consciousness is god. And there it is: absurd and absolute multiplicity.

In the beginning, the void was lighted by an immense burst of laughter.

. . .

The particular is absurd. I have seen – in conditions which I will describe shortly – geometrical figures and inconceivable movements.

I saw all that with glaring clarity. Now I can see everything in that light. At the instant when I understand a mathematical proposition, it appears to me divinely arbitrary in its own light. I said it before: the world turns inside out before my eyes, my eyes turn back into the dark of my skull, the absurd is clear.

Then my gaze overturns in me centuries clad in iron. I exist, and my ancestors had no choice but to live, and the price paid for it all was that logic which would, in an inhuman realm, seek in its own void some reason for being. I'm sometimes nice enough to provide it with some reasons; but my laughter kills it.

. . .

Yet it's not enough to laugh. The perception of the arbitrary excites man's fury and so revolt is inevitable. That formidable heredity of machine-builders is bent on making me believe that the world exists as is, clearly, seriously. Speaking with a bit of sincerity, I don't really see it clearly at all. A flower? Why does it exist? And what does that mean? Why does anything exist? No, no, the age of 'Why?' is not a thing of the past. They tried to make me believe also that a multitude of consciousnesses existed; that I was conscious of myself at the same time you were all conscious of yourselves. No, as long as that belief doesn't appear to you at least for an instant to be the most monstrous of absurdities you will remain unable to take even one step toward yourselves, you will be shadows.

. . .

The particular is revolting. But I who watch you taking your revolt seriously can still laugh. Is there then nothing that can be done if everything is ludicrous? Of course: abandon that accidental but inevitable fury and then take it back as an idol-breaking force; it will be one more way of laughing, that is, of negating; and while negating everything, if you break something – hearts, hopes, gray matter, palaces, statues, intellects, governments – just remember that that wasn't your intent (otherwise, there would still be reason to laugh!), and that the tears, the blood, and the cries are the necessary effects of a desperate race on an endless track, of a forward dash which denies the goal.

. . .

All will have to be negated, for the absurd *will be seen*. The act of negating will then become the only reality, and the negated object will become the symbol of negation. Mind is active when it negates. Affirmation, if not simple consent, acceptance without thought and dependent upon animal reflexes, is merely ridiculous. 'Who are you?' 'I am Joe, your next-door neighbor.' If whoever asks such a question were to think about the meaning of the answer, he could not help but burst out laughing. I think that affirmations are generally not premeditated. What am I? Make a list of all the possible positive predicates, and I'll always answer, 'That's not it.'

  . . .

This refusal, wherever it is encountered, is first the great *Laugh*. It's the most concrete approximation I can suggest of the distinct act which I request everyone to perform. By constantly making use of a word such as '*negation*,' whose original meaning may have been more precise, I fear I might portray this operation as an abstract pantomime of speech, an empty vocal pattern. And to make sure you don't backslide into your philosophical 'knowledge,' I will say, rather, when speaking of systematic doubt, 'sarcasm' or 'systematic derision.' Now there is scarcely reason for me to worry any longer that you will confuse this Laugh with joy.

Here we approach the mystery of separation, of negation, of the Laugh which I said was primeval, contemporaneous with the existing world.

  . . .

The act of negating separates, throws all appearances into the world of forms, into manifestation. Man cannot perceive what he consents to be. Any form is indeed somehow knowable, and thus is an object. Now, an object is that which is not me. The objective world is thus that which is thrown off as one progresses toward oneself. But since the representation of the negated object conveys nothing other than the act of negation within particular conditions, all that 'exists,' being the self's reject, happens to be the symbol of spiritual progress.

To stop saying 'I am not my body' is to sleep; from that point onward, the body is no longer represented.

  . . .

It is unusual to read or hear anything other than foolishness, nonsense, or rather pretentious *flatus vocis* on the subject of sleep.

Here I don't want to issue any 'personal opinions.' I'd rather confront you – yes, I'm still talking with *you* – confront you with what is, and to persuade you to say, in simple terms, what is happening. It's not up to me to describe what you see as long as you look *purely* and *simply*. I can maybe, just maybe, prompt you to open your eyes.

Look, for example, at the pitiful spectacle of a psychologist searching for consciousness. He says 'my consciousness' as if it were something he could possess. Who is 'he'? Who is possessed? And who possesses, if it isn't he who is conscious? These people's science is so empty that even laughter runs out of breath. Just listen to them talk on about the unconscious. Challenge them all the way, and they will think they are expressing a thought, a clear thought even, an unquestionable truth, as they articulate always without laughing the sentence, 'In deep sleep, I am unconscious.' Now ask them what the word 'I' means in their postulate. Watch their jaws slacken.

. . .

Since consciousness is in no way representable but is only the *act* of representing, what is meant when we speak of several consciousnesses? How do you distinguish one from the other? You can only say that consciousness is grasped in various forms. I create all forms – I evoke, rather, all forms through successive negations – and I become conscious of myself in each of these negations. Such is the only possible point of departure for any self searching. The absolute I'm working toward can thus be determined only by negation.

. . .

Reflection is the daughter of scandal. Scandal, the moment I open my eyes; scandal, this consciousness, one and many, identical and changing; immediate and mediate also – when I think of the *other*. What I know the most immediately, the most indisputably – this primal clarity comes forth through dazzling absurdities.

You didn't consent to fall back into sleep; provoked by this scandal, you took up the challenge. You've begun to peep at the rudiments of this absurd clarity of consciousness: an act of renunciation, of self-*abnegation*, through which the pure subject cognizes itself as distinct from what it denies that it is.

Reflection begins now, and distinctions take form. Let's linger for the time being, still bathing in the light of scandal, over a few cursory images of the road to follow:

. . .

By the same act, the subject grasps itself free of any determinations, and at the same time the forms which it takes on are brought forth; the subject is distinct from its forms and yet tied to them as a word is to its meaning. Hence the absurdity of that very separation. Yet without it, no consciousness, no representations. To respond to this new challenge, which will be unceasingly renewed, it will be necessary to *rejoin what has been separated without falling back into the primeval slumber.*

Separating sulfur from mercury joined by nature as *prima materia*, purifying them both and then uniting them again is the crux of the alchemist's Great Work.[4] Sulfur, fire and male, that which impregnates without undergoing change, is individual consciousness shedding light on diversity; mercury is water and female, that which receives all forms, itself the universal Form of all that consciousness denies. Human alchemy is no different; its basic method is the same.

At this juncture, the waiting starts for the second birth, the one spoken of in all the ancient wisdoms. Man will attain self-mastery and self-renewal; he will be what the Hindus call *dwidja*, 'twice-born.' Immediately must he separate the finest dazzling point of unitary self-same consciousness, absolute light, from its awkward cloak. It's only by stripping himself in this way that the cloak can become visible. That's why I said 'separate *immediately.*'

. . .

But my voice resounds in a chaotic desert. Argumentative answers arise: 'But, at least, we'd like to know what we're supposed to do.' I said *immediately*, with no techniques, no go-betweens, no detours, and especially – especially – without at the outset pondering the possibility of the act: locked into the realm of the *possible*, you'd find yourself hemmed in and would quickly slide back into deep sleep.

You will view your own remains only subsequent to each of your suicides. No one can die for you, no one can teach you by means of human speech the way to proceed, nor the goal, nor the means, and so I seem to be talking in a void, and yet can men not send out signs of life as a way of helping each other to avoid sleep?

. . .

Each man will thus put his own transformation to the test. Like the chrysalis: if at first it wanted to think 'I am . . .,' suddenly in the momentum gathered as if by an eternally planned miracle it's now the butterfly thinking itself into a new wrapping, a more fragile yet still opaque cloak; and the thought crystallizes, 'I am, I am . . . But wasn't that me before?' That's not the only surprise: wait till it goes up in smoke and ashes in a candle's flame. Could it have suspected this? Yet such is its allotted fate.

You can see I'm not being lyrical about what that crowd of phantoms calls 'life,' but rather about its dissolution. Ah, yes, you still haven't finished dying from real life!

. . .

There's no *way* to take the first step, it simply *must* be done. Do I have to repeat the famous 'Credo quia absurdum'? The absurd is the only believable thing. I go forth in the dark, the real night holding forth no hope for sunlight, for the infinitely distant goal is in the heart of darkness. I go forth, and my bump against the night lights up the path taken, where reason sprouts and is clad in surrogate light. Any one deed taken as is, at its most real and most conscious degree, is said to be absurd in the language of logic; but taken from within, it escapes its own ghostly empire. That is why, if I believe in what I know clearly, I believe only in the absurd.

Pataphysics[5]

I have spoken of the Vision of the Absurd in self-discovery. But it must enlighten all representations of its cruel clarity and thus become a moment in the apprehension of the world.

I willingly name this moment of knowledge 'Pataphysics,' because for me it gives due recognition to Alfred Jarry's book, *Exploits and Opinions of Doctor Faustroll, Pataphysician*. Some of the French chuckled upon reading this book. But rare indeed are those who have understood the real import of Jarry's *humor*.

Because – since I deem it necessary to relive this first burst of con-

sciousness and to be identified with the moment of knowledge personified by Faustroll – I maintain and I know that Pataphysics is not
a simple laughing matter. And if we pataphysicians often feel our
limbs shaken by laughter, it's the dreadful laughter from facing the
clear evidence that each thing is precisely (and how arbitrarily!) just
as it is and not otherwise, that I exist without being any and every
thing, that it's grotesque and that all defined existence is a scandal.

This laughter's shaking is for the body a blast of bones and muscles
torn apart by the great wave of anguish and screaming love piercing
into the last inner intimate atom, and so what! And so, with that
cosmic smack, there go pieces of pataphysician jumping inside the
guy's skin and pouncing on the appalling lies lining indefinite roads
in space and springing at length toward chaos; the individual who
has cognized himself within the whole can well believe for a moment
that he will scatter like a dust so homogeneous that it will spread like
a dust filling an absence of dust in no place, at no time: he explodes,
that lucky Earthling, but the all too solid skin, the elastic sack holds
him together and puckers only at the most flexible parts of his face,
makes the corners of his mouth rise and his eyelids slant upwards,
and distended as far as can be, it all suddenly contracts and snaps
back on itself at the same time the lungs fill up with air and then
empty out; thus bursts forth the rhythm of laughter, cognized and
sensed in oneself just as clearly as in the eyes of another laugher. Each
time he thinks he's going to burst once and for all, the laugher is held
back by his *skin*, I mean his *form*, by the bounds of his own particular
law of which form is the outer expression, by the absurd formula, the
irrational equation of his existence which he has not yet solved. He
constantly bounces back at that absolute star that pulls at him, never
getting to equipoise, and heating up from all the incessant impacts,
he turns maroon, then cherry-red, then white, and shoots off boiling
corpuscles and bursts again even more violently, and his laughter
becomes the mad rage of wild planets, and the gent snaps something, yocking it up like that.

   . . .

Pataphysical laughter is the keen awareness of a duality both absurd
and undeniable. In this sense it is the one human expression of the

identity of opposites (and, remarkably, in a universal language). Or rather it signifies the subject's headlong rush toward its opposite object and at the same time the submission of that act of love to an inconceivable and cruelly felt law which prevents me from achieving total and immediate self-realization – the submission, that is, to that law of becoming according to which laughter is begotten in its dialectical forward march:

> I am Universal, I burst;
> I am Particular, I contract;
> I *become* the Universal, I *laugh*.

And in turn, becoming appears as the most palpable form of the absurd and again I rush out against it screaming another guffaw and with this dialectical rhythm which is the same as the panting of laughter in the thorax, endlessly I laugh now and forever and this tumbling down staircases goes on and on as my sobs and hiccups shove each other forward; the Pataphysician's laughter, whether deep and mute or shallow and piercing, is also the sole human expression of despair.

. . .

And facing the faces most similar to mine, those of men, this despair turns in on itself in one last spasm and, with my nails digging into my palm, my fist closes so as to crush a phantom egg from which, if I could bring myself to believe it, a desire to teach might sprout. No, I intended only to state *what it was* for those who knew it already, those who already have laughed that laugh, just to let them know now what I'm talking about.

You who have settled into this sun of madness, this impossibly real flash of supreme lucidity, you can hear the great pataphysical voice of Faustroll, and you can no longer believe that Jarry was a madcap jokester, nor that his Rabelaisian wit and his Gallic saltiness . . . 'Ho hee, ho hee,' answers the abyssal echo of the Lying Bishop of the Sea;[6] that is the only response, the *enormous* response such an insinuation would deserve.

The metaphysician has infiltrated the pores of the world and the evolution of phenomena under the cover of body-gnawing dialectics, the prime mover of revolutions. Now, Pataphysics '*is the science of whatever exceeds metaphysics, be it in itself or outside itself, and extending as far beyond metaphysics as metaphysics extends beyond physics*' (Jarry). Dialectics once galvanized matter. Now it's Pataphysics's turn to pounce on this living body and to consume it in its fire. We must expect in the near future the birth of a new age and to see a new force spring up from the outermost ramifications of matter: voracious thought, gluttonous, respecting nothing, demanding neither faith nor obedience to anyone, but brutal in its own clarity and scorn of logic, the universal Pataphysician's thought which will all at once awaken in everyman, breaking his spine with convulsions and laughing and laughing and guffaws ripping the guts out of the oh-so-smug eggheads, and what a hellish wailing in the mildewed funeral vaults where we finally finish getting civilized!

. . .

I can give here only a few hasty forecasts of the predicament into which Pataphysics will plunge the various modes of thought, action and feeling of the lettuce-heads – I almost said 'men'!; I hope to reveal next, for example, the discovery I made of the Pataphysics of love and of a statistical method which allowed me to plot the curve of 'normal man,' which is no mean fit of laughter. For now, please allow me simply to draw slightly aside some curtains in order to reveal to you the following horrors – they're really a scream:

On Pataphysics in general. 'DEFINITION. – Pataphysics is the science of imaginary solutions; it attributes symbolically to contours alone the properties of objects described by their virtuality' (Jarry). It is the knowledge of the particular and the irreducible, thus the reverse of physics. Now, the existence of the irreducible is another aspect of my existence as a discrete being, a contradictory existence since I know myself to be part of the One. So I cannot know the irreducible except by becoming the All-in-One. Hence it can be glimpsed that Pataphysics cloaks a mystery whose perspectives it discovers in a concrete form. These few words will require hundreds of volumes to be properly elaborated. I would point out nevertheless this *revelation* from Jarry: 'It will study the laws which govern exceptions and WILL

EXPLAIN THE UNIVERSE PARALLEL TO THIS ONE.' This 'parallel universe' is the inside out world where the dead and the dreamers go, according to primitive beliefs; it's the hollow mold of *this* world; put this world in its mold, and nothing's left, nothing hollow, nothing extruded, just one unified whole. Consider, if you will, this Joe Blow[7] here and all the attributes by which he is circumscribed. From the complete knowledge of this Joe Blow, one could deduce the knowledge of all the rest of the universe by virtue of the principles of causality and reciprocal action. Similarly, remove in thought this Joe Blow from the world without changing anything else: you still imagine him right where he was, because from the knowledge of the universe minus the Joe Blow it is possible to deduce knowledge of the Joe Blow. Both relationships are symmetrical and reciprocal, and you can thus weigh the Joe Blow against the rest of the universe. Getting this idea into your head will help you get a firm footing in Pataphysics. To know X = to know (Everything $- X$).[8]

Formal logic of Pataphysics. – Pataphysics proceeds by means of *pataphysical sophisms*. The type of sophism used in Pataphysics is a proposition which brings into play syllogisms in a nonconclusive mode, but which become conclusive as soon as certain terms are changed in a manner which, as a matter of fact, the mind grasps as quite obvious; this change leads immediately into a second change of the same definitions which again renders nonconclusive the modes of the syllogism being used, and so forth indefinitely. And the object of pataphysical knowledge is none other than the very law governing these changes. Pataphysical thought processes, rather than progressing according to the relationships of extension between terms, are endowed with an instantaneous and fluid reality for the actual comprehension of concepts; they are able to slide through that dimension of reasoning which everyday logic reductively conceives of as a single immobile point. The reality of thought moves along a string of absurdities, which is true to the great principle that *whatever is self-evident cloaks itself in absurdity as its only means of perceptibility*. Whence the humorous appearance of pataphysical reasoning, which at first glance seems ridiculous, then on closer examination seems to contain a hidden meaning, then at even closer range becomes indubitably ridiculous, then again even more profoundly true, and so on, as the clarity and the ludicrousness of the proposition go on growing and mutually reinforcing each other indefinitely.

Mathematical Pataphysics. – Mathematical proofs conducted according to this logic will prove to be extraordinarily stimulating. There is no need for me to look for any better example than the magnificent calculation '*of the surface area of God*' at the end of *Faustroll*.

Pataphysics of Nature. – Pataphysics is a mockery of science more instructive than science. To my mind, the following items originated in the spirit of Pataphysics:

The theory of natural selection. ('This animal is as it is because if it were not as it is, it couldn't exist': this type of demonstration posits forcefully the irreducible nature of individual existence and traces the vicious circle of science through *reductio ad absurdum*, which is a specifically pataphysical device, even as it escapes from it. In summary: the irreducible is absurd; therefore let us reduce to absurdity in order to prove that which is already clear);

The discoveries of Jagadis Chandra Bose concerning the nervous system of plants: he made them simply by contemplating some vegetation and *then* he invented devices which were supposed to allow Western scientists, if at least they proceeded in good faith, to verify his discoveries;

The description of water offered by 'Faustroll smaller than Faustroll' (*Faustroll*, Book 2, 9), etc., etc.

Pataphysics in the industrial arts. – Not to mention *the five-hole button* and countless inventions of that ilk, the manifold peculiarities owing to purely human whimsy among manufactured objects are an inexhaustible wellspring for pataphysical discussion. Since Pataphysics as knowledge is the reverse, the exact mirror opposite, of physics, it can have a powerful effect against attempts to streamline work when applied to the flow of production. What about the influences governing the choice of such and such an embellishment which no one will ever notice on a railroad car baggage rack, or of any other gratuitous detail of some everyday nondescript object? What will all these forces which remain randomly scattered among all kinds of workers be capable of producing some day if only they are coordinated and made conscious? Such considerations open vistas onto a tremendous future for economic and social Pataphysics.

In more general terms – since I can give only a very limited idea of the fields open to this great laugh's devastation – the stuff of Pataphysics is the 'irreducible.' Now the irreducible is irreducible only because a reductive effort – that is, an attempt at synthesis in the immediate present – is presumed. The only attempt at immediate synthesis I can know directly is my own consciousness. So Pataphysics moves awareness from an abstract and universal insight to a particular individual consciousness in the present moment, that is, to a given potential for synthesis or to a particular level of the mind's absorption of the world. The irreducible thus appears finally as the imprint I, in my current state, leave on the world. And so Pataphysics will measure, in the various areas of knowledge, of action, of the arts, and of human societies, the extent to which everyone is stuck in the rut of individual existence. And it won't be just for the fun of measuring! For in this light, spines will be shaken; and minds, tossed between those sophisms' parallel surfaces from laughing to sobbing, will mirror each other infinitely. And suddenly despair will descend upon them. The way out will just have to be found.[9]

The man who has always accepted everything is as though he were sleeping. Nothing is imprisoned in the sleep of a rock. But human sleep isn't eternal; it is always on the brink of yielding. I say that the first step is to awaken absolutely so as to deserve to sleep like a rock, in a sleep transmuted into universal consciousness.

. . .

Man will have to find himself dazzled in the fury of 'No!' and his throat swallowed up in the flames of 'Why?' This will be the awakening. Scales will fall from eyes which will then behold all tyrannies.

For the man thinking up storms of doubt, blasphemies, and kerosene for the temples, it is time to take up the iconoclast's hammer and apply it to the blind face of reason, immemorial language raped, its expression ground to dust, words cast to the wind: 'All is to be challenged?' With all logic thrown off, why not believe in the unreasonable? Since any reason for believing is a waste, why not believe in insanity? Anything superstitious, anything magic will find fertile ground in this ravaged mind among the ruins of that old Discourse. Marvelous dialectics will blossom, blooming from purely artificial seeds concocted arbitrarily from start to finish. On a throw of the dice, a metaphysics will be erected: a reason to be burned alive! Ah! at last the whole range of dementia cast to the thousand winds of doubt!

. . .

Man acts. For him, it's time for the ravaging desire for liberty and guns aimed at the guardians of established order; arson and terror, and blood flowing faster than tears. Innocent as a volcano. All forms of violence unleashed at the slightest provocation. Each man becomes a hurricane, a maelstrom of natural forces. Yes! he's lost control, but he's waking up. All will be desperately lost in this sudden bedazzlement. Man makes light as he strikes out in all directions – against the skulls of those who oppress his body, his heart, his mind; against the barracks, against the churches. He makes light, and so what if he can't see it yet? He's done with sinking into the sleep of popular consent. He turns around and inside out. He has said 'No!' and he explodes.

. . .

Certainly revolt satisfies a need for violence that has simmered for too long under the iron hand of society. It will be said that revolt fulfills at least that goal and that the desire for liberty is a goal in itself, since there's no stopping once you've started. Stopping would mean getting wrapped up in new chains.

But the energy unleashed by revolt is not inexhaustible; the physiological phenomenon of fury is subject to the laws of fatigue and aging. If the rebel continues to live, if he manages to escape the clutches of established order – and also his own clutches, which, turned back against him by external duress, seek to deal his despair the final blow of suicide – a point will come when you see the violence of his muscles die and the mask of wrath melt on his face. That's where I lie waiting for him. There's no way you can count on a man unless he gets to this point.

If he merely stops and slides back into the status quo, he doesn't interest me any more; he has just confirmed that his revolt was no stronger than his physical endurance. It's perhaps not completely impossible later to see him once more break away from the new steady state in which he let himself become paralyzed; but if it's only to spend the rest of his life going back and forth between fits and stops of revolt, he is scarcely any less dead in my eyes. Arriving at revolt's critical point, man has reached the ceiling of 'the social animal'; the laws of organic life dictate that no one can live for an appreciable length of time in a state of insurrection against all organization. Between the violent destruction which he or others impose on his body and passive, spineless surrender, the third way of freedom is narrow indeed. If a man finds it, he will break through that ceiling where so many revolts come to die. Others, if the collision doesn't break them apart, bounce back down like a toy balloon and go on floating back up and back down; and chances are, one day they will stay put on the ceiling or burst and fall, pitiful pendulous skinbags. And you can sleep just as deeply stuck motionless on the ceiling as lying in a heap on the ground. Whatever the case may be, the rebel who cannot get beyond this unstable point, this supreme ordeal, is a finished, done man, wiped out in every sense of that tough term.

. . .

Ah, but that other one! What a miraculous strength he has, and what is its name? . . . What concentrated force there is in its germinal essence! It has survived victorious through the dilemma, even after the visible revolt has vanished! For this force, the impulse to revolt was only a biological reaction at a particular moment, a specifically human moment.

He knows he wasn't in it for his own or for humanity's pleasure, nor even for the satisfaction of any desire; he wasn't going for any utopia, nor for any heaven on earth; now he desires no paradise, no transhuman bliss; and all this sets him off from so many two-bit rebels who, weary, get their consolation from promises of heavenly reward. But now, pushed off with no definite hope and no limit to his hope, he still continues on his way. It was only by accident that this hapless malcontent – yes, he – had worn the mask of revolt; from now on, he can appear however he wants. Having traveled by hindsight the visible leg of his trajectory, on he goes, and we're not sure whether we can see in his eyes that nearly invisible star shooting off into infinity. His body has perhaps struck a balance with other bodies, but that's not the point: why should *this* body concern him more than any other? He is no longer of this body which *our* thinking conceives as separate, individual, and alone.

. . .

I've outlined the path which links two opposite extremes and, as such, have taken a first step in the descriptive science of the *a priori* forms of spiritual progress; we call this science Metaphysics. At first, we come to our own awareness of the universal Scandal; consciousness, upon awakening, realizes that the Absurd is the one and only thing that is clear. Then, on behalf of that first intuition of the absurd, we proceed via our acquired understanding to a critique of all our modes of knowledge. As concerns action, we go toward an attitude of absolute revolt against all the forces of ontological inertia, against all reflexes, customs, rules of conduct, and moral laws. This attitude, once ripened, would lead to complete nihilism and unleash hosts of destructive forces; it must, I repeat, be proposed as an extreme case. The contradiction it conceals, like any idea taken as an absolute and removed from its correlatives, would move any rebel straight to suicide. Yet no one can claim to be making any real progress if not capable of producing within himself that initial attitude. The man who wants *to be* must first sense within himself that violent backlash against the current of sleep and lethal human lethargy, that recoil from all his inclinations; he must even have let his hands start to follow the stormy forces of destruction. This is a time, usually associated with adolescence, of total anarchy in every area: on the level of society, a penchant for nihilism and terrorism; on the level of physiology, a door open to all the destructive instincts, all forms and variations of the suicidal impulse – a penchant for self-inflicted mutilations, for the slow destruction of the body through drugs, for self-castration. All these inclinations, whose deepest roots give equal rise to their own opposites, as they are correlatively tied to them by nature's immanent dialectics, become exposed to the light of day and coordinated by revolt's pivotal about-face, which, while it lasts, turns them into signs of quickening consciousness.

A man truly living life to its fullest must sense as latent within himself all the great legendary and historical rebels. As a brother to the Sades, the Lautréamonts,[10] or the Rimbauds of this world, he should claim as his ancestors the Asuras and Rakshasas, the Nephilim, the Titans and the Giants, the rebellious angels and the Lucifer of Hindu, Judaic, Greco-Roman, and Christian mythologies; he must be a budding Prometheus, Cain, Nimrod, or Satan, the rebel of all causes – 'all' being the name of God in a nutshell – and who for some is also called Maldoror in the mythology of our age. So it is that all these great names, worshipped and accursed, are representations within the collective consciousness, which transforms metaphysics into mythology, of the dialectical moment of absolute revolt. Worshipped and accursed they are; for revolt is awakening, access to consciousness, sole Good of all goods, for which only the Good is good. But at the same time, it is an awakening to the Double, the Contradictory, the Absurd, consciousness containing the seed of its own death; a violent break with inertia and spiritual death, but also with primal unity which shatters upon awakening; and the first act in an indeterminate series of perpetually regenerated contradictions; and a warning to man that he must unceasingly renew his tremendous effort to awaken if he is to avoid falling into the void. For thus, by taking conscious possession of himself during the act of revolt, man passes the point of no return and, as long as he remains a man, will know henceforth and forever in his own present awareness the Distinction between Good and Evil; in the eternal present of that primal act, he now calls *himself* Prometheus and Lucifer.

. . .

The act of revolt, in essence, is negation; it sets in motion a dialectical process whose final term is the limit at which consciousness realizes its own status as absolute negation fully separate from the objects negated. But the *I* which is thus posited with no determination other than the negation of all determinations can no longer be called individual. This moment of consciousness coincides with the God of the 'negative theology' of Plotinus, that is, God considered from an exclusively transcendent angle, rigorously separate from anything to which a positive predicate can be attributed. That is why it's impossible to say that this body or that human individuality belongs to this or that particular consciousness; by renouncing its corporeal or social being, consciousness gives rise to the visible manifestation of revolt; once the spirit of revolt dries up, the same process of renunciation carries on, indefinite, invisible.

. . .

These two limit-states – the unleashing within the individual person of all the destructive forces and a nonindividual, unmoving, absolute negation of everything – are two metaphysical points serving as ultimate boundary markers for the future development of every revolt. The particular course of any given actual revolt can be inscribed on the line that runs from one to the other.

On this trajectory in particular we can watch the spirit of revolt evolve into the revolutionary spirit. As we have seen, revolt in its primal state conceals contradictions which prevent it from being viable: the individual acting in an individual capacity who rises up against individual identity proceeds necessarily toward his own destruction. If he wants to escape contradiction, he must understand that the things to be combatted are all those inclinations toward death, all the forces of spiritual inertia; and that he must fight them for the sake of something greater than his own individual identity if he doesn't want to fight against himself. He will find this supraindividuality in his own awareness of being human and, consequently, in the awareness of humanity insofar as it is awakening. And since this awakening, we said, corresponds to the uprising of the oppressed part of society, the rebel will have to give his individual revolt over to the revolutionary class of his era.

And that revolutionary struggle, which must not stop short of realizing its goals, will at all times have at its disposal the powers awakened by the primal act of revolt, but now tamed and channeled.

Such is the visible field of revolt and its social transmutation. But the act by which a man, in negating himself as an individual, becomes conscious of being human is an ascetic self-denial which must be unendingly repeated and pursued, leading consciousness ever closer to its complete liberation from all forms in the Universal. Revolutionary conviction is therefore only a moment in this ascetic journey, yet a moment which can endure for an entire human lifetime. And in so saying, I still insist that Metaphysics, the expectation of a possible future, would be vain and sterile if concrete acts did not intervene to give it meaning and life.

. . .

Let's not forget the great negating Laugh hidden beneath all the successive transformations of revolt. In the very absurdity of despair, which at length kills itself with the weapons of anger and violence, that cruel laugh is far from silent. It is the innuendo behind every seething act of revolt. As human appearances become calmer, a sardonic grin surfaces. No, nothing in the most furious or most coldly desperate deeds or in the most calculated revolt has ceased being *seen* as absurd. We're not talking about joy here; there is also a laugh of horror.

. . .

Self-discovery comes only through self-negation. Revolt is no more than the most visible side of absolute negation; if it is to exist in a particular moment of time, there's no getting around the fact that it needs to be accomplished.

I always deny being what I think I am. If I'm no longer in any danger of naively and unequivocally believing myself a human being, my revolt is over. In a sense it passes over into an invisible other world.

But watch out. Those challenges put forth by the absurd and by suffering have awakened you. You have rebelled. You conceive of yourself as absolute negation, and all that exists is foreign to you. As you molted an indefinite number of times, you left behind one skin after another in the extensive realm of nature. (Nature: whatever has form, whatever is an object; whatever is in your mind as a form, such as the forms of knowledge, is thus also part of that negated nature).

. . .

But what exists – why does it exist as such? Why isn't the world just *nondescript*? Once I negate it away, it's incomprehensible. Why is there still anything in particular, ah, why still such and such a flower just so in all its details? I didn't will it that way, not me! Why is it all so arbitrary? I found the absolute purity of my essence, of the Essence. But this world? What is it? That Exterior I've pushed away in an absolute divorce, more than just an absurd and indifferent corpse, is a terrifying and incomprehensible existence. It's the anguish of being incapable of reducing everything to the pure apprehension of my own self. Now Laughter is taking on tones of madness.

Once again, suffering and the absurd! Do we have to start all over again? Yes: the act of awakening must forever go on beginning. But this moment of absolute Separation is a first step. Like any moment in spiritual evolution, it has two opposed faces: on one side, it is a moment of consciousness, insofar as it is the apprehension of that pure Essence which negates; on the other, it is sleep, so long as we consent to mistake it for a definitive *state*, a resting place. The path of metaphysical experience is lined by one such *Janus Bifrons* after the other. The time has come to describe this path.

METAPHYSICAL INTUITION IN HISTORY

I've spoken of a metaphysical function of human thought and of a need inherent to the human condition. It's only logical, even necessary, that one might find in the history of human reflection at least something hinting that there may have been attempts to come up with a Metaphysics that could be considered an absolute science.

But the history of spirit is not guided by the mere tendency to think, to awaken. If that were the case, we would recognize, over the centuries, a clear and uninterrupted progress on the part of consciousness, even if it meant we then had to admit that reflection had achieved its own perfect end. If, as we observe, progress alternates with regression, it's because antagonistic forces oppose the effort we make to become aware. At the very moment an impulse toward being springs forth, the tendency toward not-being appears as well. In more precise terms, any effort man makes to provoke thought has as its immediate correlative an organized system of ways to avoid thinking. The sloth in man's essence, that inertial tendency toward sleep, is an instrument which replaces, imitates, and kills thought at the slightest onset of awakening.

A man awakens, stands up, and proclaims that the only thing of real value is the act of becoming aware: his very words will be repeated by a thousand imitating mouths; and the more violently those words portray the singular price which being exacts, the easier they will stick dry on the lips as mechanical formulas, there to cradle minds in the deepening shadows of unconsciousness. Thus are all religions born only to smother through imitation the human awakening which is their origin, their 'revelation.'

A mathematician, through an act of real reflection, makes a discovery in the realm of numbers: right away he'll invent a formula which, once learned by rote, will from then on be used to solve any number of problems without any need for thinking. So algebra kills arithmetic as religion kills revelation: both are instruments for avoiding thinking, dead substitutes for reflection.[11] And furthermore, it is a recognized fact that the number of discoveries and scientific inventions made in any particular period of time is in inverse proportion to the current state of technical perfection.

Many other examples taken from the history of human intellectual endeavor could show thought giving rise to its own false semblances, the apparatus of its own funeral; and *being*, each time it springs forth, giving strength to the inertia of *not-being*. Let's be careful, then, we who use words to express ourselves, not to confuse thought with its verbal manifestations. The history of human thinking is not limited to the history of philosophy, which studies almost exclusively the very specific manifestations of the successive moments of the awakening of consciousness in a few select individuals. If thought tends toward a *Truth*, that truth must be held as universally valid. And all men, without exception, must be seen as the possibility of that truth's *being*. No matter whether in their preoccupation with teaching some of them make public statements and become *philosophers*. I have no right not to see in any human form a potential thinker, a virtual *being* someday capable of manifesting in action. Furthermore, all human types are linked by social relationships. So it is necessary to anticipate the interpenetration of the history of thought and nonthought with the history of social groupings; and this *a priori* correlation is confirmed by observation.

Applied to human masses formed in society, 'not-being' implies the acceptance of fallacious, ready-made modes of acting, thinking, and feeling. This consent is also a loss of freedom. Because no freedom is possible for one who is asleep. Among all peoples, at all times, there are men who set themselves up as defenders of the oppressive power of all these falsifications of thought, dogmas, ideologies, traditions; ready to profit, they impose these ways of not-being on those subjected to their domination. But in so doing, they subjugate themselves as well with the same chains of sleep, and all the more since they have insured their greater security through their own exercise of power. Thus Power immediately turns back against those who impose it.

It turns back twice: security in sleep doubly binds the oppressor. You'll never see a dominant class start to awaken, realize its decay, and reform the social order; it must constantly reinforce the beliefs which bolster its power. Scarcely able to feign, in order to rule, a faith which it could not have, it brainwashes itself even as it motivates its slaves, and thus binds itself ever more tightly. The oppressed class, thereby superior, is the one most likely to become aware. It has nothing to gain by feeding these forces of slumber; its material interest is first to shake off its economic servitude and consequently to go after whatever founds and maintains this slavery. Therefore, even as it negates the soporific ideologies of its oppressors, the oppressed class, although motivated by economic privation, must encounter obliquely but necessarily its moment of awakening.

Another force which enslaves and lulls the masses to sleep is the uncontrolled, poorly exploited progress of the techniques of production. In times past, craftsmen still had some time to think. The potter who, using his feet and his hands, kneads a lump of clay, gives it form, throws it, and fires it has a vast repertory of recipes, traditions of the craft, and necessary tricks of the trade at his disposal which, true enough, let him get around the need to think. But the mud he's working balks; it has its own laws and properties which he must loyally respect and skillfully channel until the ultimate shape of the vase he wants to produce, the goal of his efforts, is realized. Matter thus continually presents him with questions which his skill and habits cannot satisfactorily answer; now and then he has to think. These days, rehashing the ravages of what is called 'streamlining' in industry is no more than a cliché. It is commonly recognized that the rationalization of work takes away from man any need or opportunity to think. A worker no longer grapples hand-to-hand with matter. He just repeats the same movement over and over. A thousand times a day the 'line' puts the same part in front of him without his having to know where it came from or where it's going, and a thousand times his hand makes the same gesture, precisely and automatically. Now a machine among machines, a worker has to put up with this slavery not just during his eight-hour shift. In the most 'modern' factories in America and now even in Europe, you can see bosses, with the help of their own in-house police, keeping a closer and closer eye on his opinions, statements, and movements; regulating the use of his leisure time; pushing him toward ever more soporific forms of entertainment; choosing the books, newspapers, or magazines he should read, the films he should see; and checking the most private details of his life.

So the modern worker is often more enslaved than the craftsman of other times who worked twice as many hours. Streamlined efficiency, which substitutes mechanism for thought, could in fact free the worker's mind from concentration on his daily task and let him make unfettered progress. This is the rationale put forth in the name of would-be social reforms by certain so-called Workers' Parties who, in league with technicians serving the bourgeoisie, organize the worker's entire life on a mechanistic model. Just as a sensitive machine is greased, cleaned, and protected, he is judiciously assured the lowest level of material security needed to get from him the highest possible output, in such a way that capitalism can, by exploiting him, extract the highest possible profit. With this systematic exploitation of the human beast's productivity, the bourgeoisie can cut back on the growing numbers of wage earners, who are now reduced to unemployment and poverty. Society recognizes and pays attention to these workers only to the extent that it fears the potential explosion of their anger. This is how it's possible to talk about the well-being and comfort enjoyed by workers in the United States: chains perhaps forged from gold, but weighing that much more heavily on bodies and lulling dazzled minds to sleep.

Yet, even though the man-machine theme has become a commonplace topic, something is often left out of the discussion. Whereas in the era of craftsmen, producers remained more or less isolated from each other, now the mass oppression of workers, crushing individuals, lowering them to the level of cogs in the great economic machine, creates among them bonds which will become slowly but surely unbreakable. And once this human mass has clearly understood its class solidarity and its impulse toward freedom, its awakening and its destructive potential will be equal to the weight now crushing it.

The Absolute . . .

In order to exercise his reason, his judgment, and his will, man needs to believe in an absolute which is real being and highest truth and supreme value all in one. Somebody points out a passerby in the street, the first to come along. His answers to a few questions show me he hasn't a clue that such a notion exists, because, as is the case for the majority of men, analyzing the way his mind works is the least of his worries. But whoever would contradict me by bringing up this everyday example proves that he also is deluded by language: the words 'absolute,' 'being,' 'truth,' 'value,' which he knows how to use, instill a sense of security in his organism, and the absence of anxiety when he pronounces such words makes him think he understands their meaning; in fact their mere mastery reassures him enough to spare him from thinking at all. But let's dig a bit farther into the words or the silences of the uneducated man, into his judgments, his tastes, and his sympathies, however unpolished his way of expressing them may be. We'll always find nascent systems, trial structures, and attempts to base all mental acts on a cognitive principle more or less clearly set forth as a singular absolute. Most often this common basis doesn't even have a name; if it does, it's sometimes expressed by one word, sometimes by another. But in every case, provided we start with judgments and preferences revealed by observable behavior and then study their variations by tracing their vectors, we will see that the lines converge more or less exactly on a common point. This point represents the being and the absolute value which is at once the end, the basis, and the immanent driving force of all this man's mental acts. Generally, this point is not unique, and as concerns his aspirations, his choices, and his decisions, the individual obeys just a few more or less explicit precepts and rather haphazardly structured rules which are held, each in its turn, as supreme values and realities.

For my part, I name as *absolute* whatever I cannot doubt even as I doubt everything; and whatever exacts complete sacrifices from me even as I sacrifice completely. To the questions 'What is?' and 'What is it that matters?,' it always makes me answer, 'It's nothing I can name.' The only principle which can be clearly thought of as unique and absolute is the *supreme negating principle*, the perpetual refusal of consciousness to be anything in particular; it is self-denial absolutely established once and for all. Because, I repeat, nothing *is* and nothing has *value* except for consciousness as it acts; and in essence, that act is negation. More precisely, the only thing I can call absolute, the only thing worthy of the name, is *the limit which is the goal of the unceasing effort made by awakening consciousness.*[12]

But in order to grasp this notion as a living truth and not just as a simple abstract concept, one must effect in one's own mind the dynamics for which the absolute is the limit-term. This requires *thinking*. And the law of psychic inertia, which we have already noted, must instigate in opposition to this requirement of consciousness a countermovement toward unconsciousness. Man may well have understood, either truly through individual experience or indirectly through hearsay, the necessity and the worth of the concept of *absolute value*. But he forgets that necessity and worth *belong to* consciousness in its dynamic actuality. And the more he insists on retaining in his mind the concept of the absolute, the more the inertial forces of his sloth bring counterforces into play able to persuade him that he possesses the concept of the absolute simply by thinking it, with no need to perform the slightest act of consciousness. The most potent and unfailing of these forces is the use of a *name*, which, when repeated as often as necessary, takes the concept it originally signified and replaces it with an acoustic façade. The name on one hand, and, on the other, a certain sense of assurance or visceral conviction were at first tied to the same concrete movement of consciousness toward the supreme moment of reality to which we attribute the name 'absolute.' The concept expires if consciousness doesn't recreate it at every instant; but the vocal act of naming and the state of visceral satisfaction translated into thought as a feeling of certainty remain tied one to the other; a stable physiological relationship has formed between them and gives them the outer appearance of thought. And, of course, any word is able to play this role, be they the ones I've used or all the others.

Whenever you decide to talk about the Absolute, about Being, the Good, God, the Real, the True, just try this experiment: blank out all these words from the sentences you utter while imagining with all your might that you have no idea what they mean, that they no longer even exist, and that from now on there is no way of finding any others that can replace them. It is likely you will often shudder on the brink of unconscious chasms in your discourse, now wide open without their verbal lids. And the effort you make to fill in the void, thinking and recreating the slumbering concepts, is the same one that every man must demand of himself at all times if ever he wants to know and be something real.

And even then, what I'm saying in the preceding discussion presupposes a real thought as the starting point of all these phantom thoughts. Most often, the reality and the value of an absolute are affirmed only on the grounds of hearsay; so, right from the start, there's only a vague hint of knowledge. All manner of educational influences are brought to bear: family upbringing, school, catechism, reading (whether it's from books on philosophy, pious works – or newspapers, for that matter), conversations, sermons, public speeches, theater, films. Under the influence of these media, the combined forces of sleep inertia on the individual level and a tendency toward conservation in society at large instill durable links within human organisms between certain words and certain physiological dispositions; completing and reinforcing the illusion, the words *thought*, *consciousness*, and *reflection*, as vocal phenomena, wind up linked with the indeterminate feelings which correspond to these organic conditions. These correlations are established in individual bodies by various means of collective education and social institutions; they are thus about the same for all individuals, allowing for variables such as family, religion, profession and so forth. In their totality, they form what we could call the 'collective ideology of society,' provided we remain extremely careful not to designate a *thought* by this expression; because, quite to the contrary, this system, built on the cadavers of thought, is what structures the conditions within which man can live without thinking. Rather, true collective thought would in fact be the violent negation of this death machine, necessarily in tandem with the destruction of the institutions which manifest collective ideology. This awakening can be nothing less than a reason for revolution.

The Word 'God'

Physiology and sociology alone could thus explain in the majority of cases how the word *God*, as it is heard or pronounced by the human individual, induces a state of serenity, joy, exaltation, or fear; the actual concept doesn't even have to enter in. Furthermore, for anyone who hasn't had the real experience of the notion of an absolute, several names can take its place and drive the coenesthetic disposition which will be deceptively named 'certainty,' 'faith,' 'worship,' or 'grace.' In this way, a first series of counterfeits of the absolute is set up. All these names are its direct substitutes; at first they are meant to signify it, but they quickly replace and kill it. It would be easy to draw up a list of these names by choosing those which refer to the absolute considered:

as the highest form of *existence*: Being, Supreme Being, God;
as the highest *value*: the Good; or, for some, Beauty, Truth;
as the highest *moral act*: Virtue, Sovereign Good;
as the highest *authority*: the Lord, Divine Law;
as the highest *power*: the Almighty;
as the highest *cause*: the Creator;
as the highest *end*: Beatitude, Deliverance, Union;
as *intelligence*, and, finally, as *will*, as *adorable*, as *love*, as *venerable*, and so forth.

And let's not forget the very name '*Absolute*,' which is the 'highest' in general. Moreover, it is always more or less consciously understood that the absolute referred to by one of these particular facets is absolute in any other sense as well. Such will no longer be the case for the second series of substitutes which we will now briefly consider.

I could name these new semblances as *second-order substitutes*, *substitutes from degradation* or, better yet, *substitutes from incomplete self-denial*. Man continually goes beyond his own limits through successive negations. If he wants to remain conscious, he must negate at each step, each time as though it were the first, the individual form through which he apprehended himself the moment before; by so doing, he is forced to conceive the limit-notion of a consciousness which absolutely negates all individuality.

The nature of language and, moreover, the form of philosophical discourse require me to present in a general manner and in abstract terms something which has no actual, immediately perceptible reality except in a particular individual life. That is why the dialectics of 'self-denial' may appear to be a purely intellectual operation. The act which I denote (because I'm hunting for a general and understandable means of expression) by the words, 'I negate myself,' can be evinced through a great variety of actions other than those of speaking and writing. A man who silently devotes his life to the well-being of another, who gives up his pleasure, his peace and quiet, his health for the benefit of some reality greater than his own person, any man who practices self-sacrifice, whether he calls it this, that, or nothing at all, realizes an act of self-denial, the driving force of the progress of consciousness.

For example, if by his attitude or his actions he denies that what is worthwhile in him is his individuality, he will assert himself as the representative of a collectivity; to the extent that he follows up on his initial negation, he will attribute true being and value to wider and wider collectivities: family, trade association, nation, race, humankind. Each of these realities can in turn stand for the absolute. This is how the series of degraded substitutes for the absolute takes form, each substitute inspiring in men, according to their level in the scale of sacrifices, feelings of family loyalty, professional honor, patriotism, racial pride. And, depending on the outside observer's own level of self-denial, these feelings will appear as noble, if they are rooted in a sacrifice to the wider collectivity, or, in the opposite case, as ignoble. Each of these relative self-denials is good or evil insofar as it is opposed to a lower or higher degree of sacrifice. The brotherhood of man, created by rejecting true being and highest value within each human being in general, is rarely surpassed; among the masses, it stands for the feeling of substitution which least betrays the sense of the absolute. It is in like fashion, by appealing to the brotherhood of social class, that the proletariat will be able to struggle most effectively against all inferior semblances of reality and to come to an awareness of its revolutionary function.

Even the feeling of nationhood which, in comparison to the consciousness of simply being human, becomes chauvinism and generates hatred and wars, can be, insofar as it is a living reality, the only force capable of awakening an enslaved people, of making it take the first step on the path of revolution toward an ever higher consciousness. The example of the oppressed nations of Asia shows it well: for the sake of their own nation, the Annamites[13] began shaking off the chains of French domination. But we also see the other side of the coin: in China, the sense of nationhood, having furnished strength for awakening and liberation, became like everywhere else a tool of slumber and oppression. This historical law, one simple instance of the principle of correlation between the powers of awakening and slumber, suffers no exceptions.

Each one of these degradations of the absolute can thus correspond to an awakening of consciousness at a particular moment in time; once the moment is past, it becomes an inertial force. But even then, for this to be true, each successive attribution of supreme reality to wider and wider collectivities has to have been the fruit of real experiences. Most often, men recognize the reality of a particular collectivity as the absolute to which they must sacrifice everything, because this is what has been imposed and repeated and taught to them; then all that remains in these illusory derivatives of the absolute is the capacity to conserve order and induce slumber. The oppressive power of a collective ideology is tied to social structures; society by itself manages to establish its inertial force in the form of institutions which allow it to maintain itself and, especially, to impose a phantom of the absolute on its members. The educational institutions, the papers, the Churches, the prevailing opinions, the official moral dogmas are just so many forms of a society's tendency to persevere in its own 'not-being.' A nation, for instance, sets itself up as a moral limit which individuals, in their own self-sacrifice, must not overstep; if too great a number cross the line, the national reality is in great danger of perishing. Men can allow themselves lower limits: they can die for the honor of their family, their trade, their village; the nation has nothing to fear. But it is in great peril once a sizable number of individuals recognize some other collectivity as superior and more real – such as the class of oppressed humanity, for example.

All the fallacious substitutes for the absolute and all the various forces of social oppression continually intersect. So if the collective consciousness continues to consider the absolute which it names *God* as the highest reality, the ruling establishment, if it wants to maintain its prestige in the eyes of the people, must convince them of its equivalence with the divine principle. In primitive monarchies the king, at first, is God (as was the case for the Pharaohs of Egypt). Later, in so-called 'divine right' monarchies, he is the direct and sole legitimate representative of the temporal power of God on earth. If then the people wake up, they will engage in a struggle against both facets of power: the powers of the crown and the spiritual authority of the Church. Once this revolutionary period is over, the forms which had driven the upheaval of popular consciousness will in their turn produce a new ideology, a new agent for slumber in the service of new oppressors: like the 'immortal principles of '89,' a living reality in the time of the Revolution which turned into the foundation of the patriotic bourgeois ideology of the capitalist 'democracy' of France.

The study of these reciprocal influences, which I mention only in passing, will later form the basis of the science of social evolution. As it is plain to see, this will be a dialectic founded on the first metaphysical intuition: the act of conscious realization in tandem with a correlative tendency toward slumber. And the structure of this historic movement of thought will follow the scale of limit-values realized successively by the forward march of consciousness as it considers each limit one after the other as an absolute. Repeatedly freeing and shackling itself, humanity could achieve liberation only in a society organized in such a way that no single ideology might be imposed without the unceasing supervision of all the people; a society consequently in which no man or no class of men could separate from the rest of society and thereby establish a dominant position by means of a counterfeit of spirit. This postulate, this hypothetical (but necessarily conceived) limit can eventually take us from the study of social data to the sociology which some probably will want to call 'teleological.' But rather than a knowledge of social ends, it will furnish a description of current factual tendencies while necessarily keeping in sight implied yet clear-cut limit-states; the ends and means of social transformation will thus partake of the same description, thereby eliminating any suspicion of 'finalism' or of social 'ideals.' This science will gradually draw its own outlines when we have deleted by thought all forces of oppression and slumber. Once this negating work is done, there will remain the task of noting and describing the surviving positive tendencies; and like mathematicians working on a functional variation, we will define its limits. The overall system of these limits will form the sole legitimate plan of what we can imagine as an *optimal society* – a veritable *concrete ideal* – because the limit-state of a concrete variation must be conceived as concrete. This plan, which will join and encompass that of the theoretical society which we postulated above, will be as far removed from *utopia* as the calculation of a limit-value differs in algebraic analysis from some vague and sentimental anticipation.

. . .

It's the *phenomenon of religion*, by which I mean the *phenomenon of mysticism*, which has produced the purest and clearest forms of metaphysical intuition; by extension, it is this same phenomenon which has also given birth to the most fearsome forces for the beclouding of thought and the enslavement of peoples. The awakening of consciousness, whether driven by a religious impulse or by any other factor, is always accompanied by a movement toward social liberation; but the absolute offered to human consciousness quickly degenerates into a hollow sham which becomes a tool and a symbol of slavery and death. We therefore have the best chance of finding the clearest expressions of metaphysical experiences in religions at their embryonic stage, in heresies, in eruptions of mysticism; and also in any struggle against the roots of established religions, instituted as systems of social oppression. Among all peoples and in all ages, we will see the same relationship between the two contradictory functions of religious 'revelations.'

A metaphysical teaching is faithful to real knowledge if it is rooted in the immediate act I called for at the beginning: any mind wanting to remain awake (that is, to *be* itself) must incessantly go beyond its own limits through an indefinite series of abnegations; it has an *active intuition* of this progress by the very fact that it *makes* it. Now, nothing has being or value except in regard to an act of consciousness; what's more, a being or a value unfounded by a conscious act would simply be a mediated being or value – that is, abstract or virtual. (If you've been careful enough to empty your mind of its preoccupations with systems or doctrines, you must realize that I'm doing my best to state what is and that my words have nothing to do with any affirmation or negation of idealism; the first requirement is to conscientiously drive out any philosophical bias.) Supreme being and supreme good must be conceived as identical to the limit-point of the forward march of consciousness. Highest being and absolute value: this is what religions name 'God.' So a theology will be the sign of a real thought insofar as it represents God as the limit-point of the progress of a state of consciousness which we experience as immediate and which is actualized by rejecting, one after the other, individual identities that are defined in broader and broader terms. God will thus be conceived as the absolute negation of every possible determination of individuality.

Ancient Hindu Speculations

Ancient Hindu speculations, as we find them in the Vedas, the Upanishads, the Bhagavad Gita, etc., express these signs of real thought in their purest form. The very name *Atman*, meaning in Sanskrit the absolute and universal principle of the 'Self,' clearly signifies the limit-state of the personality unendingly freeing itself from individual forms. Brahma, identical to the Atman, is the pure subject of all knowledge and all action:[14]

. . .

The Atman, this limit-self, is the absolute in all its facets. It is for example the absolute object of all love:

. . .

Finally, the Atman is specifically and repeatedly said to be impossible to designate except by the negation of all attributes:

. . .

Thus, the absolute Atman is the limit toward which the individual atman strives:

. . .

And this progress is observable in this life, since any man, at any time, can perform the act of abnegation which brings him nearer to the Atman. Hindu metaphysics, in its original form, has always been closely tied to experience. It loses all meaning as soon as it is separated from Yoga, the science of Union: a method developed over the ages by thousands of seekers and capable of guiding the spirit on its path, of giving it the greatest possible number of opportunities to awaken. Thus, continually prodded to awareness, the 'self' can manage to deliver itself from individual existence by becoming *one* with the Atman.

Opposite this intuition of metaphysical reality, we see one of the most powerful organizations of political, economic, and religious oppression that has ever existed in the history of civilization. The Brahman religion, a product of perhaps the brightest spark of consciousness which has ever flashed in the course of history, becomes the underpinning for a caste system and an abhorrent theocratic tyranny. This opposition explodes in the book of the *Laws of Manu*; as long as the teachings concern only the Brahman, isolated as though he were the only real man, it still preserves intact its sense of living knowledge based on an active human experience. In the *Laws*, Brahm, the impersonal absolute, the Atman, is put forth as the limit-state of consciousness progressing toward itself, as the necessarily conceived end-point of a methodical drive toward liberation which man can and must undertake immediately. But once the priest is seen as representing the superior caste, back into his social function, he is then in a relationship with the three other castes directly born from the mythological god Brahma, and also with the throng of untouchables, of pariahs, of all manner of outcastes, of offspring of forbidden unions, of all those men which Brahmanism considers quite literally as degenerate, scarcely as men at all.

From this moment on, the wonderful revelation of the initial mystical occurrence is perverted. Nearly the entire book is devoted to glorifying the power, the privileges, and the sacredness of the Brahman. Whereas the Brahman was born from the god's mouth, all the other castes came out from less noble parts; he alone is entitled to perform the fire ritual; he is pure, intangible; he is literally taboo. In their dealings with him, other men are bound by a thousand obligations or prohibitions; violations of these rules are severely and often cruelly punished. In this case, it is clear that religion is playing its double role of enslaving the people and nipping real thought in the bud; for thought, free in its origins, is subsequently smothered under lifeless dogma forced on the people to enhance priestly power, dogma of the same ilk as the superior origin of the Brahman caste. Because of this close tie between temporal and spiritual powers, the awakening of consciousness was in no way possible without a political and economic revolt against the ruling caste.

In fact, when Hindu thought does awaken from this dogmatic torpor, its expression again reaches the highest of pinnacles. And this renaissance is nearly always accompanied by an outward revolt against the authority of the priests and the Scriptures. In the Upanishads, there are numerous philosophical dialogues in which princes, Brahmans, and ascetics are brought face to face; and it is the prince who teaches, while the Brahman is portrayed as ignorant; sometimes he is mocked and ridiculed; or perhaps a wise hermit reveals his lore to the prince and sends the priest on his way.

In the *Bhagavad Gita*, the revolt against theological authority is even more clearly defined. Vishnu has taken bodily form as a Kshatriya for the purpose of instructing men. Going by the name of Krishna, he explicitly teaches Prince Arjuna to scorn the scriptures and the sterile discussions of theologians:[15]

. . .

This book, in which Hindu thought again recovers all its initial purity and power, is the fruit of a revolt of the princely and military castes against the spiritual and temporal authority of the priests.

The revolt becomes even more well-defined and open in Jainism. It found its true fulfillment in Buddhism.[16]

. . .

By rising up against the authority of the priest, he regained within himself all the concrete and universal conditions for self-denial.

Since these conditions were the same for any man, since any man's reality was in the same private act of thinking, no spiritual obstacle could ever again separate individuals into castes.

But in their turn, the teachings of the Buddha became dogma and were shrouded in theology. It's true that he never managed to prevail in his native land. If he had, the result could have been the replacement of Brahman domination by the type of princely and military aristocracy which Jainism introduced in a few provinces (???). The revolutionary awakenings of ancient India were always incomplete, because they were led by the Kshatriyas alone. It would have taken an awakening and a revolt of all the castes and the masses of outcastes to truly liberate the Hindu people.

But in Tibet, for example, Buddhism, once transformed into Lamaism, becomes an official religion with its dogma, its rites, and its clergy. In Buddhism, Supreme Good is conceived as a limit-act, an ideal attained in exchange for a human personality which has been delivered from itself; hence the reincarnations spoken of in Buddhism: those of its great saints and of the disciples of Gautama or their spiritual descendants, and those of the ascetics which the tradition holds as having attained salvation or the extinction of individuality in Nirvana.

So if with the support of traditions and dogma some individual succeeds in passing for one of the 'living Buddhas,' he can gather to himself all the respect, veneration, and awe inspired by a sacred individual, a 'taboo' being; and this is how he can secure his own political as well as religious supremacy.

In fact the priesthood in that country has the most numerous and the most powerful means for killing thought by replacing it with its counterfeit and for lulling the people to sleep, all the better to dominate and exploit them. Tibetan mystics in whom the spirit awoke throughout the ages invented very clever and very efficient techniques for dominating girls' bodies and passions at will. By submitting bodily movements to a certain discipline, consciousness could become free of them by negating them; it could then seek itself out in calm meditation. But the value which these true *thinkers* attached to the basic *act* of thinking was quickly transferred by the lazy multitudes to the techniques themselves. And so it became a *magical value*; these practices were thought to foster the progress of consciousness by their own power. It wasn't long before they were made to serve aims secondary or completely foreign to the pursuit of the Good. They were used to attain physical or superphysical powers: strength, health, sharpness of perception, etc.; second sight, levitation, and all supernormal human faculties. Hence all of Tibetan sorcery. By means of prayer wheels and beads and endless repetition of mechanical chants, the priests put individual awareness to sleep. Even if they teach in all good faith, they can in no way teach what cannot be taught but must be *done*: the act of thinking. And probably there still were – still are – priests and theocratic lords clever enough to use these techniques for the enslavement of their subjects.

This is how the type of theocratic feudal system particular to Tibet was founded and is still conserved, with the person of the Dalai Lama as the eminent focal point of both forms of power. But the dialectical chain of rebirths and deaths of religious thought is endless. Throughout the social and religious history of Tibet there are those who come forward and, by rebelling against established authority, trigger awakenings of consciousness; whence the profusion of mysticisms, heresies, reforms, and sects which make the study of Lamaism so complex. But, in Tibet, the preponderance of religion is so strongly entrenched that any conscious solidarity among the oppressed masses remains all but nonexistent. Therefore, these explosions of consciousness are usually the doing of a single individual, the most common example being a monk who breaks all ties with society, goes into the mountains, and meditates, perhaps later to teach. These awakenings of thought then often leap in a single bound to the heights of the *pure* and *simple* revelations of ancient India.

India and Tibet

Throughout their histories, India and Tibet have experienced more than any other land a tremendous abundance of attempts to *think*. And more than in any other land, the priesthood has always found a way to appropriate all these manifestations of thought and turn them into vehicles for theocratic power. By now, this turnabout should be no surprise. But we whose goal it is to awaken must try to understand why these superhuman efforts on the part of consciousness failed; our findings may be quite instructive.

All thought is revolutionary; for, being the offspring of doubt, any thought threatens to undo oppressive ideologies. On the other hand, any expression of thought can in turn become one of these very ideologies, or at least be absorbed by those which already exist.

This will necessarily be the case whenever there exists an oppressive power threatened by the awakening of consciousness. Revolutionary thought will thus be unable to achieve its aim completely unless it is coupled with a material force capable of destroying the power of oppression. Now, in the histories of Brahmanism and Buddhism, the quickening of consciousness was always tied to two major forms of revolt: the individual revolt of the ascetic who denies society by 'withdrawing to the forest'; or the revolt of the military and princely castes against the priestly caste.

In the first case, the individual, from the perspective of subjective idealism, does indeed eliminate all social antagonisms, since, being alone, he stops perceiving society. Of course I'm thinking of the most exemplary yogi, one who gets his food, clothing, and shelter (if indeed he has any) without the support of any other human, who even learns to meditate without the support of language, that eminently social instrument of expression. But neither I nor you see from his point of view. No man living in society sees from his point of view, no man can any longer pass human judgment on this one who has renounced society, who is no longer quite the basic 'social animal,' who is no longer a man. He has committed social suicide. In this case, the problem persists for us intact, and that individual revolt, however absolute it may be, has changed nothing.

But Hindu Yoga teaches the truth that what appears as the best becomes the worst when it is sought by an individual as personal satisfaction and not in and for itself and for every man, universally. The ascetics who are truly great in the minds of us social beings, those who have played a revolutionary role in history, leave their hermitages and come back among men. Some are satisfied with teaching their 'revelations' to a few disciples; these 'revelations,' if indeed they are real thoughts, can be nothing other than the upshot of a negation focusing on the oppressive dogma of caste, of class, or of the dominant religion. But, once in the public domain, the expressions of such a thought will be stolen by those in power, who will appropriate them for their enslaving ideology. Or, on the other hand, the ascetic's teaching will remain strictly esoteric, in which case we don't know anything about it, we can't use it to benefit society, and there we are again, no farther along than if he had stayed absolutely and definitively alone. No matter if four or five or more of his disciples have also performed this subjective revolt – or, for that matter, just he alone. Even so, there is a tradition carried on in just such a manner which managed to play a true revolutionary role across the ages; I will talk about it in a little while.

For now, I'm considering the anchorite's revolt only from the point of view of its momentary social efficacy, an efficacy which is nonexistent as concerns the confirmed hermit. But it could occur that the ascetic might wish to pass on his living thought to his contemporaries. Such were the cases of Mahavira for Jainism and Sakyamuni for Buddhism. They claimed to be speaking to all men on behalf of all suffering beings. But without the support of a unified, conscious oppressed mass unavailable at that point in history, their rebellious thought could inspire only a discontented fraction of society. The caste of warriors and princes used this revolutionary force against theocratic authority and then, once in power, perverted it by turning it into a new dogma able to uphold their domination.

The social action of Buddha and Mahavira, founders of religions in spite of themselves, comes down to the second form of revolt: the uprising of the Kshatriyas against the Brahmans.

This type of revolt was supported by a concrete social force. But let's suppose for the time being, and for the sake of historical simplicity, that the military caste, in the name of a religious awakening, had broken Brahmanic dogma and priestly constraints and had seized power. In Hindu society, Brahmans and Kshatriyas make up only the two most noble castes; then there are the Vaisyas, the Sudras, all the secondary castes, the impure Chandalas, and the outcastes. Even though the caste system in ancient India was less rigid than is commonly thought, these social formations were nevertheless much too distinct for the revolt of the Kshatriyas to succeed in uniting in one single revolutionary consciousness all the rest of society's oppressed classes against just the one class of Brahmans. The separation between the two highest castes was rarely absolute. On the other hand, there was an abyss separating the Kshatriyas (and even the highest three castes) from the lower social strata, which, already divided

amongst themselves, often could be used as passive and docile instruments in the hands of the rebellious princes and warriors. Once
the military caste came to power, its foremost concern was to insure
its domination over the rest of society. It needed institutions and
ideologies, those of the winner supplanting those of the loser. The
power of small theocratic communities yields to a military feudalism
or even to a monarchy. Brahmanism is replaced and, because it remains a very strong dogma, is assimilated by the ideology which
worked to break it and which becomes in its turn an official dogma
and religion. Revolutionary thought died from not having stirred up
all of the oppressed.

Of course, the social history of ancient India is too complex for
such a phenomenon to have taken place in as general and schematic a
manner as this.[17] However, the dialectic I have just sketched out can
be used as a connecting thread to aid our understanding. It should
not be forgotten that no struggle between the two highest castes was
likely to result in a particularly bloody revolution, since the barriers
separating them from each other paled in comparison to the ones
which put both of them far above all the rest of society. We must also
take into account the various invasions which were a major factor in
India's political changes, especially in the establishment of the great
monarchies.

Keeping in mind these reservations, we can understand how the
pious monarchs who protected the two 'great heresies' were able to
supplant, thanks to their religious zeal, the old priestly power and
gradually transform their small feudal states into powerful realms.
This movement surely began, long before Buddhism, with the birth
of the first Hindu feudal states, probably parallel with the anti-Brah-
man activity of some of the first masters of the Upanishads. The evolution carries on with the monarchs contemporary with Buddha and
Mahavira; for example, in Magadha, Bimbisara, the friend and pro-
tector of the two preachers. Here, the advent of Candragupta, founder of the Maurya empire (a consequence of foreign invasions),
speeds up social and religious evolution, thereby making it somewhat more complex. But the success of his most famous successor,
Asoka, is without question due in large part to the active propaganda

that this sovereign put forth in favor of Buddhism. How priceless is the protection of princes, who can turn a living thought into a religion of death and slavery! (And you – never forget this: flee the protection of your oppressor, the bourgeois; this already rotted Corpse is still a practicing vampire: with your life he wants to feed his contagious Death.)

This quick analysis explains well enough the fate of the awakenings of thought, at first revolutionary, which gave rise to the Upanishads, Jainism, and Buddhism; but it could give the impression that behind these spiritual and social upheavals there were individual intentions working as initial causes. Nothing could be farther from the truth. To predict the fate of true thought, all that is necessary is to dig into the reasons behind princely uprisings against priestly authority. We started with an antagonism between two castes – castes taken as unquestioned facts. But the reality of castes, hidden under this or that social or religious appearance, is economic to the core. The Brahmans exercised power fully in early Vedic society with its patriarchal structure. The development of the means of production in the agricultural sector, leading to the need for new means of exchange and the beginnings of commercial centralization, increasingly impelled the advent of a new form of political power. The Brahman, whose function was tied to the village community fire, was unable to break away in order to extend his power over a wider social group. He simply became an adviser to the prince who assumed this political role. The Kshatriya's rise to power amounted to the sanctioning of a new economic regime brought about by the inevitable progress of the forces of production. Since priestly authority was upheld by dogma, the prince had to break down the dogma. Now, *any negation of a dogma is an awakening of thought*. The economic revolution thus furnished by necessity the opportunity for an awakening of consciousness. We have seen that such an awakening will usually create a darkening of equal proportion, in this case because the economic revolution was not radical and affected only one part of the Brahman population.

I'm neither an historian nor an economist. I don't think I've gone astray from my resolve to follow single-mindedly the connecting thread of Clarity. I invite anyone who so desires to gather together documents on the history of any given Hindu kingdom of any given period: I know *a priori* that the guiding principle which I have just put forth by analyzing a schematic example will always suffice to explain the history of social revolutions from the economic, political, and religious points of view at a given time or place. But what's important for you to consider is this: the dialectical law according to which consciousness, as it manifests itself, constructs the mechanism of its own death is the law of all evolution. Heraclitus and Hegel proclaimed it to the world. About a century ago, it was applied with marvelous rigor to the social history of the peoples of the West by Karl Marx. Only those who might well suffer from it will stubbornly refuse to realize his clarity: I mean all those who, one way or another, take remorseless advantage of their social position in the ranks of any class of oppressors.

You who are reading me now, listen closely: think back to where you were when I started talking and how far you've come since, and realize that I've done nothing to steer you astray. I asked you to open your eyes to see clear evidence: the immediate reality of that act of consciousness whose very expression brings about its own death. I led you into what may be called a privileged land, where numerous voices across the ages have always presented that same evidence. You've witnessed the fate which kings, priests, and later the bourgeoisie have always necessarily imposed on such words. You've witnessed the mechanisms by which the products of thought were used to kill thought and to enslave bodies. I gave you the example of India, because that country has teemed with thinkers for nearly three millennia, thinkers whose voices, by their purity, have tempted and still tempt so many Westerners like you, wanting to think freely; also because in that country, the products of the acts of consciousness of thinkers in revolt have given rise to the very worst instruments of spiritual and material slavery. So you see: as long as there are men who exploit other men in the society where you live – that's what they'll do to your thought.

. . .

[Here ends the part of the manuscript which was typewritten, revised and corrected by René Daumal (cf. p. 5).][18]

So! You Want to Think Freely!

So! You want to think freely! The more you think you're expressing your own free thought, the more your words will be made into chains for you and your brothers. Be sure that there can be no free thought wherever there is a class of men oppressing other men.

But, on the other hand, there is a means, which I taught you along the way, of preserving the integrity of your language. I repeat: As long as thought is alive, it is revolutionary; or vice versa. But I showed you that your thought, if it is to be alive and revolutionary, must dovetail with the existence of a material force capable of destroying the institutions through which oppressive ideology crystallizes. But that's not enough: once the chains are broken, you will still be in danger of taking your own turn at being an oppressor, and this, as I said, is the same as going not just once, but *twice* through spiritual death. To be decisively alive and able to fulfill completely its inherent revolutionary function, your thought must correspond to the existence of the material force of the entire oppressed segment of society; again, Karl Marx demonstrated once and for all that this is the force of the entire world's revolutionary proletariat.

Now, don't be so easily satisfied by my phrasing. Remember what this relationship between your thought and revolutionary force really is. Thought originates only through the active doubt associated with negation. The proletariat is engaged in a struggle to the death, whose outcome is known in advance, against the bourgeois capitalism which exploits it. The only thought which can be considered alive[19] and completely revolutionary is one which originates from the negation of that bourgeois nonthought; and, in relative terms, a thought is alive and revolutionary in proportion to the degree to which it negates the dead ideology of the dominant class. To the extent that your thought is explicitly and strictly a negation of the bourgeoisie's negation of thought, it will be safe from any appropriation which can benefit the oppressor.

In this area, Karl Marx's work will always be an example of essentially imperishable thought; as such, it constitutes an historical moment which is determined absolutely and which absolutely determines human thought. Marx was the first to have connected his own thought to the totality of the material forces of revolution; the first, therefore, to have written a work which, in a necessary, absolute sense, cannot lend itself to appropriative interpretation for the benefit of the ruling class.[20] A social-democrat of today who supports the use of power in a capitalist regime cannot lay any claim to Marx without looking ridiculous. Whoever claims to be a Marxist has no choice but to think on behalf of the international revolutionary proletariat; otherwise he commits a deception so infamous that he sinks into the most grotesque form of shame.

Even Hegel, who revived in our time the old dialectical method used by all revolutionary thinkers, was not only robbed by the entire 'Hegelian right wing,' but was betrayed as well by himself (or rather by the bourgeois Prussian who lived inside the same skin) to the benefit of a status quo imperialism. Marx, who learned dialectics in the Hegelian school, wanted nothing more than to avenge the living Hegel against the bourgeois Hegel when he attacked the latter and claimed, with Engels, to 'put back on its feet' the master's dialectic.

So I haven't led you astray. I could have let you pursue an increasingly conscious 'pure consciousness' in an individual and sterile metaphysical search. All living thought negates that which is individual. I didn't want to let you fall asleep in a pleasant intellectual pastime. Reality is harder. You have to search, not for yourself, but for all men: under this condition your thought will be real. But right away, you realize the existence of a social class of oppressors who are ready to pounce on the first word out of your mouth; and no sooner do they suspect the existence of a thought in those words than they take over your language and freeze it among their dogma-corpses. This bourgeoisie has a favorite dogma: a so-called 'freedom of thought'! You have to realize when coping with this hypocrisy, this lie, that so long as there are class antagonisms, the only thought which deserves to be called 'free' is the one which, on behalf of the oppressed class, pursues the radical destruction of this master class.

Free thought is also true thought. I will call a *true thought* any thought which is unquestionable and imperishable, that is, a thought whose expression will never, in any case, in any way, lend itself to being used by the ruling class against the oppressed class. Thus, in the spiritual and social history of ancient India, which we have been briefly discussing as one possible example, so many different social structures either coexisted or went by in succession, so many revolutions were spawned or aborted, that it is legitimate to attempt to track down in the traditions of its past a few vestiges of *true thoughts*; we will find them by seeking out the quality of imperishability which I just defined.

At this point I don't want to dig out the living yet hidden core of the thought expressed by the philosophical literature of India; we are not in India, and since an effort of this sort can not be applied to immediate social needs, its only outcome would be a useless – and therefore wrong, false, and dead – system. Over the course of our search for imperishability, we may encounter moments and processes of thinking which were put forth by the sages of India; only then will we sometimes let those unknown men who spoke out in the past speak out again, better than we are able to, on what we have to say today. For example, we can find, starting now, precious illustrations in Hindu philosophies of the principles which have all along been informing our discussion.

The Sages of India

Something else helped to spread powerful truths in the vast philosophical and mystical literature of India, truths which were the fruit of ancient revolts and the seeds of future revolutions. The theological books themselves are undermined and poisoned by truths which negate them. I have ignored as irrelevant to the social history of the period the role of the ascetics, who, after long years of solitary meditation, would pass on their teachings to a few rare disciples. There is no way we can know anything about the level or kind of knowledge to which these men had attained. But I venture to advance the following conjecture which it is up to you to test through a dialectical study of the history of Hindu thought:[21]

We can extend our trust at least far enough to affirm that many of these ascetics were in fact truly great thinkers. And so they were great doubters. They denied all dogmas, because they recognized their power to oppress. Furthermore, they were incapable of seeking truth without desiring it for all of humanity. Some of them thus came back to society to teach men the desire for freedom; such were the cases of Mahavira and Buddha. Others went farther ahead in their thinking. They remembered similar attempts and how they failed. And they wondered why. As I say this, I cannot believe these inveterate seekers were blind, blind to that evidence whose clarity dazzles me – and I have lived such a short time and studied men and society so little: that the entire ruling class appropriates for its own benefit (and thereby assassinates) all manifestations of free and revolutionary thought. They knew that any public expression of their thought would have provided new instruments of oppression to new priests, to new tyrants . . . They didn't have a proletariat which could materialize their thought in the social arena. Some of them, probably, purely and simply dropped out, and, holding the 'illusion' of the world in contempt, died from the sublime thought: 'The truth *is*, and nothing else matters.' And then there were those who realized:

'The body? Society? Illusion, illusion. Maybe. But the pain, the ignorance, the slavery which the body and society make millions of men on earth suffer? Real, real, real! I have found the path of deliverance. But if I teach the *method*, men will turn it into a *doctrine* which will do nothing but reinforce their enslavement. And yet the method is a good one, the right one. Over the course of the ages, there will be privileged times when human misery attains its most bitter, most conscious, and thus most powerful form and demands a method by which to break its chains. I must, for the ages to come, perpetuate the knowledge which I have had the good fortune to acquire. Then there will be men who will know how to derive from this science of universal deliverance the right method for their historical time.'

The anchorite then seeks out disciples. He puts their bodies, their minds, their passions, their wills to a thousand various tests over a long period of 'initiation,' that is, of beginning and of preparation. Most of them do not withstand these tests. With kind irony, he sends them back into the world filled with useless knowledge, sure of themselves. For what he wants to test is each one's relentless propensity to doubt. The *believers* are lost, their faith is a form of sleep. Finally, one disciple, passing all the tests, persists in *thinking*. His doubt is victorious: he had nothing else to learn.[22] His education is finally complete when he renounces even his own personal salvation. At this time he understands, as the master teaches him, that he is no more than a very small speck in human evolution, a humble messenger with the mission to pass on a Method to the ages which will need it. He in turn will seek out a disciple and will pass this knowledge on to him. Now and then, those novices who listen to him and get carried away with zeal will want to record his teaching in books and make it public. But, cleverly, he disguises the awesome destructive power of his thought in a few verbal expressions so hermetic or ambiguous that not one of his contemporaries can interpret them harmfully; so that one day the ones who understand will be those whose thought can be realized only by moving the powerful lever of the misery of an entire people or class.

Such is the 'esoteric' teaching of the sages of India. It is passed on in much the same way as the initial hit on a series of billiard balls: each one, invisibly, secretly, receives and passes on the impact, but the only ones to move forward are those who have a clear path in front of them. I'm not saying that the only goal of this esoteric tradition was a long-term revolution; its goal is *deliverance*. And man is not the slave of society only; he has a body, for instance. But for whoever has really understood the meaning of the secret tradition, its only immediate goal, today, is the revolutionary struggle.

This revolutionary ferment hidden in the Upanishads, books composed by small groups of disciples, was able to play in India the same role as that of Hegelian philosophy in the West. One day or another, there will be a Hindu Karl Marx who will know how to draw out the essence of the dialectic method hidden in this literature. Gandhi came upon the scene too early to apply the theory of the identity of opposites, as taught by his Jain masters, to his country's too-recent class struggle. Another man will accomplish this necessary task. The Vedanta can provide him with a solid point of departure.[23] This system – Hindus more correctly say *darshana* ('point of view' or 'investigation') – the last of the six great schools rooted in the Vedic tradi-

tion, is a synthesis of two doctrines: Sankhya, an absolute materialism or dialectic of universal evolution, and Yoga, a technique for
individual development, a kind of scientific mysticism. Sankhya has
certainly prepared a number of Hindu minds in a dialectic science of
social evolution; and Yoga encompasses a certain number of methods whose effectiveness has been borne out by centuries of experience and which could be put to good use as a means of revolutionary
education.

It matters little whether we admit or not the scarcely verifiable
existence of a revolutionary esotericism passed down by this oral tradition. In all ages, there were always revolutionary dialecticians.
They were usually not understood and were thought of as hermetic
authors. Heraclitus came up with the fundamental principles of the
Hegelian dialectic; but it seems his philosophy remained purely philosophy, since it encountered at the time no economic forces capable
of putting it into practice. You could say that Heraclitus thought not
so much for his age as for ours. Starting in the most ancient times,
dialectics has been awaiting its appointed time. The bell has rung.

So I have cited Yoga, which teaches that whatever can be a good
for humankind becomes an evil if it is sought exclusively by and for
the individual. For example, it is possible to speak of man's spiritual
forward march; but whoever seeks this progress solely for individual
satisfaction will be truly regressing.

The school of Advaita (which means 'negating dualism') in Vedantic philosophy has preserved the trace of several spontaneously
forged truths brewed in centuries of revolt and religious fermenta-
tion and tempered in the fires of social antagonisms. The expression
Advaita itself, often translated in the West as 'monism,' contains a
verity; it signifies: 'the negation of dualism is true.' History has
shown that philosophical dualism has been a matchless servant for
the forces of religious enslavement. Any religion, insofar as it is a
means of social oppression in the hands of a ruling class, takes on a
dualistic form no matter what its particular circumstances may be. It
can be, for instance, the matter/spirit dualism of Christianity: matter is 'contemptible'; the masses must therefore resign themselves to
suffer 'materially'; their 'mortifications' will greatly edify their 'spirit.'

In the meantime, naive faith, the Christian resignation of the serf, allows the feudal lord and the priest to fill up their 'material' bellies. Yet on the other hand, proclaiming the truth of 'monism' is insufficient. A philosophical monism could still easily be twisted into playing the same role as dualism. When Plekhanov declares that the Marxist dialectic is monistic,[24] it is rather in a sense which implies *active negation* of duality. And so for the Hindu Advaita. It is not a matter of positing pure *unity*, but rather of *negating* the dualism which threatens to enslave our minds and spirit and, of course, our bodies as well. Since dualism is a force for the preservation of the bourgeoisie, *nondualism* can only be a mode of thought as lively as it is revolutionary.

The central postulate of Advaita also puts forth a verity: 'all things are in the self, but the self is in no one thing.' This formula in all its simplicity, as we can see, condemns *pantheism*, which in the West serves as a common vehicle for a so-called 'Hindu mode of thought.' By adding to it the principle that the 'self' (Atman) has no value unless it is understood as belonging to any thinking man and not to one particular individual consciousness, we condemn in the same stroke *subjective idealism*, another Western version of 'true Hindu thought.' These two condemnations lead finally to a positive outcome: things, since they do not contain any 'self' or 'consciousness,' can be seen as subject only to a determinism which is neither inside nor outside of them but whose necessity is at one with their very movement.

This in fact is the direction Hegel took in his interpretation of Hindu thought; he even managed to be authoritative in spite of the scarcity and the vagueness of the translated texts available during his period.[25] One must admit that thanks to a few crude tricks of translation and improper systematization used as a basis, it has been possible since then to establish in the West the most egregious falsifications of Vedantic doctrine, from the form of intellectual exoticism determined by who-knows-what mixture of stupidity and 'Intelligence Service'[26] characteristic of Theosophy to the intelligent and strictly authoritative commentaries of Mr. René Guénon,[27] who cleverly manages to justify a theocratic system of divine right – which moreover probably never functioned in India.[28] It's as though someone fully aware of my ignorance of German were to try to pass off on me *The Imitation of Christ*[29] as a translation of the works of Hegel. I'm sure that for a Hindu the doctrine of Advaita can only be revolutionary; it seems to me that a reactionary Advaitist must be just as basely ridiculous as a Marxist social-democrat.[30]

   . . .

I intended to apply this dialectical method to a religious phenomenon closer to home for Western readers. I would have simply pointed out as a possible field of study the Hebrew prophets whom, although they were often great rebels if not for that matter true revolutionaries, the rabbis have adroitly succeeded in assimilating and fitting into their Bible. Too bad for the Hebrew prophets. I then wanted to carry out a cool-headed examination of the two faces of the Christ phenomenon: the revolutionary Christ and the Christ used as a pretext for Christianity. I thought I could do it all the more disinterestedly insofar as I found out about Christianity somewhat late in life and only as a matter of intellectual curiosity, since I never received any religious education of any sort. But Christianity must be a particularly serious problem in the society I live in, because the violence of my reaction to this religious phenomenon determined the very form of my expression, as seen in the title 'Poem to God and Man,' which I am including in our discussion at this point.[31]

Poem to God and Man

God,
God, first of all it's not you God,
not God I'm talking to
God, I'm talking to your inexistence,
I cast my eyes straight out like stones
not at you, I cast my eyes straight out everywhere,
straight out at anywhere you're not
like stones cast out but into the void
like stray bullets

I cast my voice like a stone out everywhere
straight out and away anywhere you're not,
I cast my voice out into space, but, God,
in no place do you have ears

God, good God, good old damn Deus,
beardless,
hairless,
with nary a bristle,
You're not good, you're old, damn old,
damn old God, I'm not swearing,
old and ageless, deaf and earless,
I prithee even less.
You don't have the eye of God, God,
not the arm of God, God,
not a God foot, not a God belly,
not a God skin, God,
God without man
God without devil
God without god.

God, damn Deus in four letters
D as in Desire
E as in Enlighten
U as in Universe
S as in Stupidity

name of the name
no of inane
holy no of name of not-God
enough fooling around, louse!
here comes rage up red through my teeth
here's me looking, into the void, bashing
an eye, here's my voice bashing
an ear, here's my stray bullets, zing!
and zing squirting at a real schnozz,

at a true smacker fat and purple
or at a rotten lemon yap
or a smile like a pair of pliers. Someone.

Here he comes, he's talking to you, God,
he's praying to you, God, he's talking about God
he's putting bifocals on your inexistence,
he's sticking fake ears on your inexistence,
and he's putting long white hairs on,
hairs everywhere all around your emptiness.

God, damn Deus in four letters,
there's no way left to understand
he's hollering, the skunk, he's hollering: God, God,
here comes the padre, yelling your damn four-letter name,
here he comes with his damn yap
and his Desire to Enlighten the Universe with Stupidity.

Poor damn old nothing God!
it's not your fault you've got that dirty hairy face
white and pink and harmlessly senile,
it's that bastard who slapped on the paint,
that padre who stuck you up in heaven
with his Desire to Enlighten the Universe with Stupidity,
he's the one that smeared paint on that senile face
in his image, that sneaky old bastard,
botching and bashing hard-headed men
per omnia sæcula sæculorum.

As for me, priest, I spit in your face in the name of God,
– it's for my own health,
and it's a ritual gesture –
and I'm talking to that dead man
that tiny little dead man
– you can't see him? you fool, he's right there in your hand,
you nailed him to two pieces of wood –

Dead man my good old brother
A thousand and one times dead man;
in all lands a thousand and one times murdered
by that swarming race of rats who talk to God,

You had eyes, my good old brother, eyes that could see!
you had a voice that could wake up the thousand-year-old living
    dead
that could awaken a violent vitality in the hearts of slaves,
you had all the same stuff a man carries around,
you gave away everything,
your eyes, your mouth, and all the rest,
to your brothers so they could make themselves a God
from your wretched human remains.

You gave it all.
The man you had been was no more.
And all of a sudden you were standing face to face
with the Emptiness of God.
That evening, on the Mount of Olives,
you, the man denying your humanity,
you, by yourself, already sacrificed right to the quick of the soul,
you saw the emptiness of your own face
facing you
face to empty face, you saw God,
Ah, yes right at that instant, what a flash
what a pillar of thunder over the earth
between your human emptiness and the emptiness of God
you had killed your human past
you had killed your hope for a divine future
Then, oh yes! then only was there the sole presence, one to one,
of Man, of God,
of Man identical to God in his emptiness,
identical for no more than a moment, a single moment,
Christ, emptiness of man on the Mount of Olives,
Christ, emptiness of God on the Mount of Olives,

you saw yourself, you saw God, God saw you
in the dazzling and formless mirror . . .

now, you scum – you can scream:
right through your cassock, my fingers
are already squeezing your rotting heart,
and age-old legions of slaves,
your victims, my brothers, my gods,
are the strength of my arms, so –
so you know you're going to pop like a flea
between my fingernails – 'Ain't no good god
ain't no good god,' scum,
'ain't no good god' says my arms' human rumble,
and you took my good old brother
– no way he could avoid getting killed
once that life blew open up there on the Mount –
you drooled on his human face,
you insulted him with the name king
you nailed him up on that yard and that mast
you put in his mouth your lying words
and you blew your plague-wind at his back

And, padre, you took the helm of this Ship,
hauled along by the throbbing sails of human flesh,
across the ages,
and this Ship – you heard me: this Shee-ip,
this tremendous Ship
put together for the duration by you, padre,
the Ship called Christendom
hauled along by throbbing legions of slaves
across Christian ages,
you lent out this Ship (in return for perfectly honorable
remunerations, right, Pope?)
to kings: they brought you their galley slaves,
and then to the flies feeding on royal carrion –
for that bourgeoisie also furnishes galley slaves

(but be careful, my little padre! I think this latest batch isn't
    going to swallow your line for much longer) –
And across Christian ages
your lying word, from four evangelistic mouths
swollen from the Desire to Enlighten the Universe with
    Stupidity,
has betrayed the motionless flesh of my good old brother,
nailed up on that yard and that mast,
not responsible for your Ship, you jackal,
he who made the Emptiness of God from Human Emptiness
yes . . . but he also who flows in legions of human flesh
in the veins of my tightening fingers
and here, take this, your rotten heart as it pops,
croak like a rat.

But wait, it's not over so easily;
one kicks off and a thousand regenerate:
stay clear, church vermin.

The sail of throbbing flesh cruises on,
my good old brother's Corpse, deaf and blind,
still hauling the Ship,
the Good Ship Christendom through the ages.
He hadn't planned on that . . . But
but after all this Corpse is a Corpse,
even though I love you from the depths of despair,
man my good old brother, you're just a piece of carrion.
Your tortured body, which you threw to us as fodder,
stinks just like my human corpse will stink,
it's chewed up by millions of worms: by
Roman Catholic worms, by
Orthodox worms, by
Protestant worms, by worms
each one out-groveling the next
each one more faithful than the next
to the true and authentic purity

of the great Christian pestilence,
and everywhere, in the East under various names,
– Krishna, Buddha, Fo –
all of them the same carrion,
everywhere my good old brother under umpteen different names
you're chewed up by millions of worms
each one out-groveling the next
each one more faithful than the next
to the true and authentic purity
of the great Brahman pestilence
of the great Buddhist pestilence
of the great Lamaist pestilence
of the great Taoist pestilence
of the great universal pestilence:
the stinking odor of sanctity.

Crucified carrion, making the cemeteries bloom;
your life, good old brother, has left the Ship,
your life already shared among us all
shortly before that business with the cross,
up there on the mountain with the olive trees
where you sacrificed Man and God in the same Emptiness.
Your life is no longer this cross-bound corpse;
your life has vomited out the Ship and the entire race of
    cockroaches
who talk about God under the four-fold protection
of the holy evangelistic yaps.
Your life has multiplied in innumerable throngs
in legions of bleeding men,
always tortured by the same tormentors,
always under the holy protection of the same priestilence
per omnia sæcula sæculorum
in the centuries of divine right Royalty,
in the centuries of divine right Bourgeoisie,
per omnia sæcula sæculorum.

If the Emptiness of God was Some Thing
at that time when he negated himself in Man,
Then God you are ebony, the black flesh
which those lice called missionaries
help to die as Christians
– dozens of them for every kilometer of railway –
for the greater glory of Christian civilization,
to haul the Good Ship Christendom,
Serpentine God with millions of black heads
sliding in pain across Africa,
in you my good old brother's vengeance is ripening
and weighing itself in anticipated pleasure, and you,
Serpentine God with billions of yellow heads
bursting under bales of cotton,
under bombs dropped from airplanes blessed on departure
by a Christian hand,
living God, guillotines are being worn out
on the self-regenerating swarms of your heads,
the good old brother's blood flows in your veins too,
while plotting and anticipating the pleasure of its vengeance
through also the black and white God
who trudges all through America,
through the God with a million pale heads,
with black hands, but,
but soon red, but
but sorry good old brother,
sorry to have sullied you by calling you God.

It's your blood which swells these skinbags called men,
ain't no good god, ain't no good god,
your blood-red ocean where you'll drown finally,
ain't no good god, a billion padres
vicepadres, archpadres, bastards,
ain't no good god, your turn,
your turn for the Word
your turn, human Emptiness of God:

once the five fingers of your red hand
have wiped the world's face,
then, set up in front of yourself humanity's past
aim at the heart, and bang!
and alone, having purified the world's face
with the fires of the good old brothers' vengeance,
purified the world's face of all vermin, all that vermin
which already suspects and fears you
as the Antichrist,
alone, a being with pale, yellow, and black heads,
alone, yes, a veritable Antichrist,

– Antichrist to make that Christian vermin tremble,
all that vermin, Buddhist, Brahmanic,
Lamaist, Taoist vermin –
alone in this instant and delivered
from lies past or future,
you'll get the great miracle moving again
– but this time, by the fire of the good old brother's
vengeance, don't let the vermin regenerate –
alone facing off with the Emptiness of God,
in this brotherly
and dazzling
mirror,
you'll know

REALITY

Moreover,[32] the Marxist school of thought has treated with all due erudition the issue of Christianity's being a factor for social slumber and enslavement. Since at this juncture I'm especially concerned with pinpointing the critical moment of the awakening of consciousness which precedes the stifling influence of religion, I must emphasize the climax which occurred in the thinking of the 'Galilean agitator': until the Mount of Olives, Jesus hardly attacked anything more than the religious forms of the Jews of his time; on the Mount, as far as we can make out through the conceit or the hypocrisy or the naïveté of the apostles' reports, something phenomenal happened. What could it have been if not that 'revelation' or, rather, that awakening to the truth which, in man's case, amounts to the negation of the personal God? After that much-vaunted night, right up to his death on the cross, the Christ, either dumbstruck or watching out for his disciples, seems to behave like a robot doing 'as it was written.' This is how Nerval sees it, and he puts it magnificently in his 'Christ on the Mount of Olives':[33]

> He turned to them who, awaiting him below,
> Were dreaming they were kings, wise men, prophets . . .
> But lulled, lost in animal sleep,
> And he cried out, 'God is not! No!'
> They slept. '*The news*, my friends, do you know?
> My brow has touched the eternal vault;
> I am bleeding and broken, and must suffer for days!
>
> Brothers, I was wrong: Abyss! Abyss! Abyss!
> There is no god at the altar where I am sacrificed . . .
> God is not! God is no more!' But still they slept!
> . . . .
> . . . .
> 'Searching for the eye of God, I found only a socket –
> Vast, black, bottomless – and from this dwelling, night,
> Radiating, thickening ever outward over all the world . . .'

I suspect that at that very moment – a moment which could by all rights be called 'divine' if present times were only ripe for a revaluation of words, which is doubtful – at that very moment Jesus, not altogether conscious as yet of his revolutionary role, in sacrificing himself, his individuality, for suffering humanity and in denying the personal God, realized through an unspeakable torment the 'negation of duality,' the Advaita of the Hindus.

. . .

And still you'd go on about freedom of thought! Even when the truest, the liveliest words of the Upanishads, of Buddha, of Jesus – if they were pronounced as I presume to reconstitute them just to make it easy on you – when all these words of liberating revolt have become shackles, dogmas, prisons.[34] Today you can't be sure to speak freely and truly unless you attack the bourgeoisie on behalf of the proletariat. You can't hope to express yourself without fear of being robbed and betrayed unless it is in a society without oppressors watching over your every word. This is the goal the revolutionary proletariat seeks, but it can do so only by means of a violent overthrow of power. This mechanism which Marx clarified is so simple, so merciless, so irrefutable; as I said, it is only those who sense themselves as its future victims that tremble. Let's now suppose – not even a perfectly communistic social state, which itself is a limit-state analogous to a mathematical limit and as useless to bring up as it is to affirm as real – let's just suppose the existence of a society *consciously* moving toward communism under the diligent direction of an already enormous proletarian majority; there is really nothing utopian about such a society. The proletariat has come to power by becoming fully aware of its historical role. It needs no hypocritical dogmas, no ethics or official religion in order to govern itself and to finish the job of eliminating the residual traces of whatever has survived of the bourgeoisie. It proclaims loud and clear its conscious and precise goal. If living thoughts well up in its breast, it will not stifle them or use them as ideological masks. It will let them grow to fulfillment like the unfettered activity of thinking humanity. Having learned from its age-old experience, it can and must take henceforth the most thorough precautions so that these renascent thoughts will not crystallize into dogmas, not be set up as religions. With its awareness bolstering its confidence, it will not lack the means to remain vigilant.

Above all, the best possible antireligious educational system will have to be organized. During the revolutionary period, when religion appears as an old enemy, the anticlerical and antireligious struggle, fiercely and purely negative, is all that is needed.[35] In a communist state, men will have the leisure time to reflect on humanity's past experiences. They will remember the underhanded power by which the ruling classes set up religious ideologies by cleverly using the remains of real thinkers. Now, we may well hope that the members of the proletariat will spend a good part of their leisure time striving to think about themselves and to become conscious of what they are, but they will have to be careful that their words do not stiffen their thoughts into dogma. True, the danger wouldn't be the same as it would be in a society based on class antagonisms; there would be no oppressive class capable of turning the proletariat's expressed thought into a religion or some other form of oppression. In the limit-state of perfect communism, there would be nothing left to fear: man could 'think freely,' and these two words which adorn the bourgeois lies of today would finally have a real meaning. But we can rightfully suppose no more than a society actively on the move toward a limit-communism. In which case, any expression of thought could become, no doubt with increasing difficulty, a force for stagnation, a brake applied to that evolution.

Dogmaclastic Institutes

The remedy is always located next to the problem. Neither 'Nature' nor 'Providence' set it up this way,[36] but rather the dialectical law which states that all things call for their own opposite. We can find the very force which can nip any threatening dogma in the bud quite clearly manifested throughout the history of dogmas and religions. We will have to extract from the thinking activity of great heretics, of destroyers of religions (founders, in spite of themselves, of new religions), of numerous mystics, *not* the 'ideas' which could found a new dogma or a general theosophy just as pernicious as this or that sect, but rather the mental orientation and the methods which made them revolutionaries. We will thus arouse a positive antireligious force which will guarantee the integrity of liberated thought. At the same time, this force, negative to the core, generating consciousness, will make the proletariat awaken more and more to itself and thereby quicken its evolution. In the schools, the dialectical history of religions[37] will be taught, and the totality of human speculative activity will be centered around *Dogmaclastic Institutes*.[38]

Starting now, in our present bourgeois regime, the antireligious struggle could usefully derive strength from this historical dialectic. Providing, of course, that the effort not blind us for one second to the immediate revolutionary goals. Here I address in particular sincere seekers of thought. Not scientists, philosophers, theologians, and artists who, consciously or not, uphold the bourgeois order through the individualism which motivates their endeavors. If you're really a seeker of thought, you've now understood that as long as one class oppresses the other, you will be a slave; that the realization of free thought is the same thing as the realization of a communist society. You can't think without willing the victory of the proletariat. For thought to be expressed without being betrayed, it must be explicitly founded on class struggle. You'll never be able to separate your thought from social struggles and, in the final analysis, from economic contradictions, as long as any two classes of society are fighting to the death. Thought will not be capable of moving toward a victory over itself except in a communistic society. Even if you don't think that real communism is possible, you can't get around the fact that it's impossible for you to express yourself freely in any other social form. If you're not attracted to communism, you're at least pushed in its direction by the contradictions of bourgeois society. The walls are closing in around you more and more every day; if you write a book, if you paint a picture, your bourgeois readers and admirers will praise you for reasons which are the exact opposite of those which determined your creation. Only one door is still open, and, whether you hope or not to use it as a way out, you can't help but go in its direction, unless you decide to sell out to the oppressors or commit suicide – to betray, in any event, your thought and the revolution.

I've taken you from the immediate act of 'realization' to the recognition of the necessity of the class struggle. As concerns the details of this struggle, as for the general outline of capitalism's evolution, of its collapse, of the proletariat's takeover, of the establishment of socialism, you could legitimately accuse me of sketching them in too arbitrary a fashion. But the science of the mechanics and methods of revolutions has been defined once and for all.[39] I don't have to defend the work of Karl Marx; it can defend itself and with what authority! It proves its own truth by itself, and history confirms it as well. When it shies from making detailed predictions concerning its application to the proletarian revolution in this or that region of the world, it's because in all that, there is indeed an unpredictable element; but, in each particular case, there will necessarily be men who concentrate about themselves the current revolutionary consciousness; they will define the manner and conditions in which the proletariat will come to power: the Russian proletarians had Lenin.[40]

And you might be surprised, if your mind is still cluttered by the mechanical habits of sectarian philosophical languages, that, even though my point of departure was the consideration of disinterested research into consciousness, I have now reached a point where I accept doctrine. You're going to accuse me of taking off from 'idealist' premises just to end up in 'materialist' conclusions.[41] You'll try to find out by what subtle trick of reasoning, what paralogism, or what sophism I was able to perform this pirouette. You'll maybe remind me that Marx himself reacted violently against this sort of trick, against the 'idealists' of the Hegelian left, against Bruno Bauer[42] in particular, who based his social dialectic on 'immediate consciousness.'[43]

Only someone who hasn't wiped his own slate clean of all philosophical biases can level such blame. I've performed no pirouettes. My language conceals no tricks. Right from the beginning, I've refused to take sides in the abstract debate which opposes 'idealism' to 'materialism,' in the purely philosophical and sectarian meaning of these terms. Philosophy, by twisting the meaning of words, by giving them contradictory meanings and values, has in the end deprived itself of a clear and exact language. Thus, all systems should be put aside so as to start all over the job of thinking by attempting to *describe what happens* as exactly as possible.

I didn't start from an 'idealist' position. I noted that the only thing I can grasp through immediate active intuition is consciousness. Whether he affirms or denies the 'reality' of things, whether he claims to be a 'materialist' or an 'idealist,' no man can refute me. If later I note that this consciousness has contents and represents various changing objects to itself, I would still add nothing to this description by stating that these contents are 'illusory' or 'real.' But my thinking really progresses as soon as I perceive the irreversibility of this relationship of contents to container; for consciousness, which, rather more than just a 'container,' is the very means by which objects are represented, can not be thought of, except by means of a hollow abstraction, as contained by things. Since it grasps itself, consciousness necessarily sets itself off from the existence as such of things. Later, you and I will try to see how consciousness gets located in things in the form of a dialectical necessity. Such an attitude is very difficult to maintain. It is the same as that of Hegel's *absolute idealism*. Consciousness can maintain such an attitude only if it remains rigorously oriented toward the universal, if it is sought out, not for any particular individual, but for all men; and, as a corollary, it must not stop noting the obvious *existence* of things as such. Indeed, as you've seen, if you want to think for all men, you must find an incorruptible mode of expression; and you can't unless you take the economic structure of society into account. There is no reason to be concerned about the *free expression* of thought in the case of subjective idealism or, more simply, the case of an individual thinking only *for himself*; in this case, thought seems to become much easier to exercise and to express; but, in fact, as soon as this occurs, thought dies. In his *Philosophy of Right*, Hegel sets about thinking *for himself*; he is only too happy to apply *his system* to justify the existing social status quo; the dialectician of change, the successor of Heraclitus suddenly stops at a particular moment in social evolution, and, against all expectations, seems to conceive of it as being a 'good' and definitive state! At such points, Hegel is no longer an 'absolute idealist.' He's just an 'idealist.' He becomes an individualistic thinker. Next to the real Hegel, who is and always will be the 'Titan of the human spirit,' as Villiers de l'Isle-Adam[44] calls him, another Hegel appears, a clever philosopher able to serve the imperialism of his country with the mortal remains of his thought. As for the master's disciples, they all fell completely back into individualistic philosophical pursuits, into the 'idealism' which only Karl Marx ever condemned. Due to its blindness in the face of social antagonism, this philosophical 'idealism,' whether it was declared to be 'left-wing' or 'right-wing,' in time became powerless in the struggle for the social liberation of thought. In reaction, Marx had no choice but to declare himself a *materialist*, even as he retained Hegel's dialectical method and antidualist attitude. This is how dialectics could be said to be 'set back on its feet.'[45]

'Materialism,' first and foremost a fighting word, expresses the condemnation of everyday idealism and of all individualistic philosophical pursuits; it equally condemns all dualism, even if this dualism claims to be 'materialism.' Mr. Le Dantec is a materialist, or so he says;[46] but his 'materialism' is only one half of a dualist doctrine. He implicitly admits the duality of mind and matter, but through ignorance of the dialectical method, and in order to obliterate the contradiction inherent to such a system, he prefers simply to omit mind. This is why Mr. Le Dantec as a 'materialist' is an admitted reactionary. But Marx's doctrine is set forth as a 'dialectical materialism,' and that expression doesn't lend itself to confusion. Marx got it right the first time: it is henceforth impossible to construct a materialist dialectics of social history which is not Marxist, just as it is impossible to construct a geometry of experiential space which is not Euclidean.[47]

The leftist Hegelian 'idealism' which Marx attacked aimed to construct historical dialectics on idealist premises; the dialectical sociology of Hegel was simply a part of an idealist philosophical system. On the contrary, when I asked you to give it a try, I wanted to prove to you that it is impossible to think really if you refuse to think for all minds; and that you can't think for all minds without running up against the obvious existence of a dialectical determinism of social antagonisms. To realize that, there's no need to bring in some abstract system to represent the world; in fact, it's essential to clear out all philosophical biases.

A 'free thought' is not a thought free from the 'choice' of this or that form of expression, as though indifference were any guarantee of freedom. We've seen that if a thought is really alive, the form of its expression is determined by the necessity incumbent upon it to escape the enslavement which the ruling class threatens to impose upon it. In the final analysis, the means of expression of thought is determined, on one hand, by the biological conditions of language and its state of historical evolution (which simply provide the possibility of expression), and, on the other hand, by the economic contradictions of society, which determine the existence of this or that form of expression. This is the price that language, if it recognizes this determination, pays to be fully conscious, to understand the necessity of its own manifestation; only in this sense is it *free* or, rather, *freed*; also in this sense only the 'materialist' thinker is free. There is no other freedom but this. 'Free will,' the 'freedom of indifference,' is only a phantom of liberty. It is of the essence of thought to think all things as determined: the language of the thinker just as any other object.[48] Now, thought itself is not an object of knowledge; real thought is defined as that which cognizes the process of determining; the determined is not the conscious 'I,' but rather the forms through which it apprehends itself. A materialism which sought to determine – if these words could in fact have any meaning – the knowing 'I' would only add to the known world a new material principle, one so far unheard of, a 'thought' which would be a thing; this materialism would be *false*, for *conscious thought can not be said to exist* in the material world. It thinks, on the contrary, the necessity of the world.[49] Thus, the true materialist dialectician is the sole thinker who is really free. Only from the moment when he has clearly recognized himself as this real thinker can a man begin the true pursuit of being 'ever more conscious,' not for himself personally, but generally, for every mind in actual operation.

. . .

The same dialectic which determines the history of religions must be found at the basis of all manifestations of human thought: art, ethics, philosophy. The history of science will be more complex; scientific thought is in fact a continual compromise between two types of human activity: the technical improvement compelled by the latest necessities of the ever-evolving means of production and trade; and the purely speculative tendency which makes the scientist become now and then a philosopher and awaken from his technical work to check its direction, like the sailor who must become an astronomer to verify his course.

In all these areas, we will find the same rigorous law: all thought springs forth from the negation of a nonthought, of an established dogma; and the forces of social oppression construct their dogmas using the dead expressions of true thoughts.

The history of ethical ideologies is no more than an extension of the history of religions. After a certain number of centuries of struggle between human thought and religions, despite the ability of that Proteus called religion to take on a thousand various forms, the numerous blows landed on him can sometimes weaken his resistance. This happened in Europe in the modern era. The quick succession and the coexistence of various antagonistic sects, all laying equal claim to God, gradually generates, however, a certain skepticism concerning them in the minds of a growing number of individuals. The moment a large enough number of men stop acknowledging religious values as absolute, it becomes dangerous for the ruling class to shore itself up on these shaky dogmas. It's death for State Religion and the beginning of the separation of Church and State.

For a long time, all the attacks aimed against religions were launched in the very name of God. So in any transition period, you'll see enemies of the ruling class, enemies of all religion, still invoking God as their authority; whence Robespierre's 'deism,' whence the cult of the 'Supreme Being.' But such an ideology didn't connect with the force of large revolutionary masses; so it couldn't last. As it went about setting itself up as a dominant class, the bourgeoisie developed a new ideology which was supposed to replace State Religion, an ideology nevertheless flexible enough to encompass the still very powerful current of religion which it could also frequently exploit – which explains the bourgeoisie's need to give precedence in its ethics to tolerance and freedom of thought. The 'secular ethics' which was thus established can be divided up, roughly, into two levels. On the first, there are principles of theoretical ethics, borrowed mainly from the thinkers of the eighteenth century and summed up by a few famous words – Liberty, Equality, Fraternity, Republic, etc. – which quickly took on a sacred aura and the intense 'taboo' by which any social order protects itself. These principles were crystallized into the 'Declaration of the Rights of Man and Citizen,' and their great merit resides in their still semimystical emotional power which in turn is related to the great flexibility with which they are applied; likewise, the bourgeoisie is able to justify or condemn whatever it pleases in the name of a Justice which is no less abstract, metaphysical, and unverifiable than monarchy's God. The second level of official bourgeois ethics consists of precepts, rules, and duties which are more precise, more practical, and better adapted to the social order to the extent that they stem directly from the economic structure of the nation and the conditions under which it developed. From this we get all the duties and all the biases revolving around individual property and the family; finally and especially, the internal and external political conditions which allowed the birth and growth of the Republic clustered around the word *Patrie*, our native land, and created a focal point of sentimental forces which allowed the ruling capitalists to send millions of men to slaughter on the battlefields and to line their pockets from these massacres.

I don't claim to be able to sum up in these few words the enormous mesh of infectious dogmas cast over the people by the so-called democracy of the bourgeoisie. I simply want to put out a reminder that the ideology of a class in power can quite easily not present itself as a religion, can even claim to be independent of any religion; but this is just an indispensable smoke screen, and, in reality, 'secular ethics' plays the same role in the French Republic as religious instruction. In general, schoolteachers, traitors to their own people, lay waste to children's minds with the sacred words of Native Land, Duty, Justice, Field of Honor, as priests do in like fashion with their own equivalents: God, Sin, Providence, and Paradise. Even so, it appears that in the wake of the most recent carnage,[50] a certain still small but growing number of educators has become aware of the abhorrent hypocrisy of these words and has sensed its solidarity with

the masses, the only people capable of cutting down the class of pil-
lagers which defends its treasures with the weapon it calls the 'secular
republican ethic.'

So where in that bourgeois ideology can we find what is eternally
alive and revolutionary, that real value which we necessarily encounter in the wake of any negation of an oppressive dogma? If you have
that much trouble finding it, it's because you've forgotten this: the
French Revolution was the political sanctioning of an economic revolution begun a long time before it, with the introduction of machines and factories for the production of goods. The ideological
Revolution had also preceded the political Revolution. In the effort
toward destruction and liberation, in the destructive and critical
powers of the great writers of the eighteenth century – that's where
you'll find *thought* eternal. But watch out, these are nonetheless
Janus-faced figures: they're strong and tall as long as they attack the
old social order and political and religious tyranny; but there on the
ruins of the *ancien régime*, they already all too often let the future
bourgeois dogma take root. And so it had to be; for, not detecting
the seed of the proletariat among the people, they couldn't know
that men could later be oppressed by their liberating ideas.

We had to wait for Marx and his successors before we could find
men conscious of the oppressive power of any ideology controlled
by a ruling class; the positive result of their destructive and revolutionary work was not a new ideology, but a method: in science, it is
called dialectics, and in social action, class struggle.

Why Write a Book?

– Okay, but when do we get to the experimental metaphysics?

– My, but you're in a hurry. You still haven't figured out that we
have to start from the beginning? I would have led you astray if I had
let you believe in the possibility of a 'free' thought independent of
social problems. You're seeking something I'm seeking too. We still
don't know what that thing is, nor even if finding it is possible. But if
after this dark picture of our economic slavery you keep on seeking,
your ailment is incurable. So I see that the only thing I have any right
to say to you is: I don't know whether you'll find anything, but I

know your search will be in vain and even harmful to humanity as long as one class of men exploits another.

– Fine. But all you've talked about up to now is religions or their substitute, class ethics. Religion is a social phenomenon, so it's not surprising that it's tied in to the economic forces which govern human life. Religion can't be between you and me. If we pursue our search privately, there's no need to fear that it will be turned against human freedom.

– You're right. But you, you I'm talking to, I'd like you to be multiple, as many of you as possible. I'm writing a book, and I think I'm responsible for whatever good or bad it might do. If men used it contrary to my intention, I could only accuse myself of having written an ambiguous work subject to misinterpretation.

– Okay, but why write a book?

– First, formally, your question is lame and is subject to a refutation *ad absurdum*. If the fact of writing or not writing a book were contingent, you'd have to be in a position to ask me one or the other of the following questions: Why do you write? and Why don't you write? Now, if I hadn't written this book, you wouldn't have read my words, and you couldn't ask me that first question. The only one you can ask me is: Why do you write? So, by asking that question, you admit that I needed to write this book. (I'm developing this argument, which appears to be purely formal, just to get used to thinking of what exists from the angle of its necessity.)

Next, all individual speculation quickly encounters a ceiling, provided it doesn't explode so it can pursue its own ends in the universal. Or, just to start again back at the beginning of things: I become aware of myself by negating myself; I know myself in the end as 'pure *I*,' as the essence of what constitutes my individuality. And in spite of that, I keep on perceiving the world from a particular point of view. Henceforth, I'm shut up in a subjective idealism which I can no longer leave, unless I perform another negation. The only thing left for me to negate is myself as an individual. Then, the realization becomes a universal value, and a new progress is possible. But I must know that it is possible for any and all men. Starting then, I am determined to devote all my energy to provoking other men to an awakening so that they begin seeking with me. Writing this book was one of those tentative beginnings.

– Yes, but in the course of history, there have been individual seekers; and all philosophers claim to be searching for a truth having validity for any human mind.

– They claim to, yes. However, not one pure philosopher has succeeded in directly touching, awakening the human masses. One individual's metaphysics is always abstract speculation. You need go-betweens to enliven the thought of a philosopher for the people; and from that moment on, it is subject to the same laws as any collective ideology.

– And what about you? Do you think you're going to make the human masses think, directly?

– No, unfortunately! To a large extent, I too am a philosopher. I'll already consider myself quite lucky if I succeed in shaking up a few intellectuals, a few seekers who still think they are unconnected to social conflicts, or if I can make them feel disgusted with their hollow individualism and at least win their hearts and minds over to the necessary revolution.

– But aside from that, do you therefore look down on the specifically philosophical part of your work? You see all philosophy as abstract and pointless; are you going to continue to write philosophy?

– I didn't say that exactly. Always applicable to philosophical activity is the dialectical[51] law of consciousness as the negation of the negation of consciousness. Any philosophy has two sides: On one, it negates and destroys preceding philosophies, religious and ethical ideologies gone to seed as dead dogmas; in this sense, philosophical thought is alive and revolutionary, more or less radically. On the other, philosophy builds; insofar as it is constructive, it can be the more or less disguised reproduction of dogmas which it forgot to tear down; it can also be the intellectual and individual expression of an existing social order, reflecting indifferently the economic contradictions of a period as they are spontaneously and collectively expressed: religion, class ethics, national pride, etc. In both cases, philosophy is conformist, reactionary, dead, and asphyxiating.

– Philosophy is thus reduced to negating if it wishes to be lively?

– No, I told you, at the beginning, that a positive cognition had reality and value only as far as it was the anticipation of an act of consciousness.[52] Thus, a scientific law is true and valid insofar as it posits the conditions in which I can note, using my eyes, a given phenomenon. The philosophy of science, an anticipation of that anticipation, can thus constitute a science – a potential one, indeed, but a valid one as well. As for metaphysics, it is valid as long as it postulates the conditions necessary for a concrete experience of consciousness itself. In these conditions, philosophy can construct and remain a valid form of knowledge.

– So let's get moving! What about that knowledge?

– What? You think we're not already there? Didn't I clearly establish for you the necessity of leaving behind the individualistic quest as a primary condition for an awakening of consciousness? And another condition: taking sides with the oppressed class and in no way blocking its revolutionary function?

– That's not fair. You stated the conditions. I'm expecting the expectations.

– Watch out. Wanting to win everything without being aware of all the conditions, you just might lose everything. Because there are other conditions. And the very ones I pointed out to you are quite difficult to realize. One day when I sketch out the overview of the anticipations of the progressive awakening of consciousness (if this task proves possible), at each word I utter, I will risk being misinterpreted, robbed, and taken over, all for the benefit of a dogma of slumber and slavery. So I must take as many preliminary precautions as possible. And I tirelessly repeat:

The experience of the consciousness which I will attempt to anticipate will never be possible for whoever hasn't first realized certain conditions; in particular, for whoever hasn't done everything he feels capable of doing for the true revolutionary liberation of spirit;

this metaphysical cognition, today, will therefore not be valid except for a small number of men, exclusively for those whose revolutionary force it will in no way weaken;

it will not be valid for humanity as long as humanity is divided into antagonistic classes.

– So you admit that your 'metaphysics' could weaken in many men's hearts the potential for revolutionary action?

– If I were even the slightest bit worried about it, I'd stop writing now. I'm committed to expressing myself[53] in a language such that men incapable of grasping the revolutionary essence of my thought can neither comprehend nor use it in any way; for them, it will simply be useless. But knowing that it can awaken the thought of a few others, I don't want to back down from this fearsome responsibility.

– So . . . some form of esotericism after all?

– If you wish, but an overt, self-declared esotericism, one that doesn't hide a truth for being 'dangerous' (just how can a truth be dangerous?), but which on the contrary protects truth by expressing it in precisely chosen terms; one which would prefer that truth not be grabbed by those incapable of grasping it, rather than letting the opposite of truth be read into the words which express it.

– You were talking about the recognition of the necessity of revolution as one of the conditions of spiritual progress. What are the others?

– One thing at a time. But just in case you still don't mind meditating on this obvious truth, which is much less banal then is usually thought: The conditions under which man, the 'social animal,' shows that he's thinking are of two categories: social and biological. Thinking man is linked to two types of natural mechanisms: the body's biological mechanism and society's economic mechanism.

– So finally who are your anticipations of self-denial meant for?

– For those who will be born in a future society, saved from class battles, for those we'll never see. They too will have unforeseeable struggles to confront; new conditions will be stipulated for the progress of their consciousness. But what I can predict is that they will have one particular condition of existence in common with us: *the human body*. And with nothing more than that machine, they'll have their work cut out. Our anticipations won't be enough for them; but, sought after by us according to the principles we have just set forth, they will be universally valid and, I hope, useful.

– So you admit you're a philosopher, but you try to be one in the best sense of the term. And what's left of the philosophers we're familiar with, the ones who've thought and written since the beginning of history? Is it possible to find positive and eternally valid results in their work, insofar as it negates dogmas or anticipates concrete experiences?

– Yes, but only if you study their work in depth at those points where it brings forth instances of thought meaning nothing except in relation to previous instances. You know, once a truth is expressed, its expression can be used to kill any truth. And also, any truth can be stated by two successive philosophies in two ways which are contradictory yet equivalent in relation to that basic realization which brought it up in the first place.

– But then, how are we supposed to derive some one-pointed and positive doctrine from all these contradictory expressions?

– You're *incorrigible*! It's still human thought talking out of your mouth. You want pat truth written once and for all in a few convenient books? So that those who own these books might be the wise ones and not the others? Why not adopt right away the prayer-wheel system?

No, because truth is an act. Truth is made. You don't think the truth, you think *truly*.

And besides, you know all about the miserable results any attempts at eclectic philosophy have always had. It's not a matter of choosing among doctrines. That choice would always be more or less arbitrary.

But here's what we can do:

You've no doubt suspected and later you'll have a clear demonstration that the historical development of philosophies reproduces a general reflection of individual speculation. If you wish, it's an intellectual corollary of Haeckel's onto-phylogenetic law.[54] As our thought unfolds into its own research, we'll come back to certain spiritual moments which this or that philosopher dedicated himself to expressing. The history of philosophy will be revived so as to feed our own thought's self-expression.

– But, at any rate, you're going to set up a doctrine; you know, a simulacrum of thought.

– No. When I try to find out how these philosophers expressed

this or that living instance of thought, I'll always find several seemingly contradictory doctrines; I'll show that it was like this because,
since spiritual reality always comes out of negation, this philosopher
awakened while negating that dogma, just as this other one negated
that other dogma, all according to the times in which they thought.
Philosophy's real meaning will be born out of the clear presentation
of these contradictions.

Metaphysics

No philosophy can predict what a man will think, and so can't determine what a man must think. Each man will think whatever is before
him; and that is unpredictable. All that can be done is to set forth the
conditions without which a man cannot think and especially the conditions within which he cannot think.

It's up to each one of us to know what must be thought. That way,
no dogma can replace what reality will be for us at any particular
moment in time. No dogma to blind us. I can hope only to suggest
methods for fighting against the inertia of sleep. There's no way to
give each man a preview of his way toward liberation; but I'd hope
to shut him off to as many ways out as I can; he'll bash into all the
doors leading to slumber, slavery, and spiritual death. Thanks to this
sort of demonstration *ad absurdum*, he'll have to see the only un-
closed door. I can't tell him where it will take him, or even if it will
take him somewhere. But he'll at least know that everywhere else
there's death and that if he doesn't move there's also death.

In fact, I've already posited a first positive and clear condition
without which any metaphysical quest would be in vain: in the final
analysis, I'm talking about a complete adhesion to the revolutionary
will of the proletariat.

– Yes, but that's an outer, foreign condition to the essence of
thought. After all, the class struggle is not metaphysics.

– Not metaphysics? What do you mean? We're men. We each have
a body and an existence linked to the existence of other bodies by
economic relationships. Any man who awakens realizes the existence
of the body and of society. Now, this first awakening is the first metaphysical act. If metaphysics, as the anticipated progress of consciousness, doesn't take the clear and distinct discernment of that double
necessity as the point of departure, then to hell with metaphysics!

– If you're sincere, you must indeed be saying, 'To hell with metaphysics!' You must admit you're giving back to this word a value it had lost.

– Probably. But I think I've done it explicitly enough. Spirit no longer has any language by which to express itself. All the religions and all the dogmas serving our oppressors have for a long time turned the language of truth inside out. They have stolen and murdered words, leaving behind nothing but empty carcasses which can be used for any end. Since these exploiters of words are of the same class as the exploiters of humanity's labor, the Revolution will wipe them out. I'm anticipating somewhat in advance the era when at last people will be able to speak freely without wrapping each word in ten pages of protective explanations. The word 'Metaphysics,' as I say it, is enslaved language's cry of revolt.

APPENDIXES

I've put aside the utopian issue of the future of science in a communist society. Since such a society does not yet exist, I can only hope that it will destroy the one type of mechanism that there is to destroy, the one which, implanted in men's brains, mechanizes and enslaves their thought, their reactions and their initiatives; that it will reestablish science in the honorable position which befits it; and that such a society will recognize the necessity of more efficiently ferreting out mysteries and replacing them with a knowledge which is an art of living, a culture both real and whole. It is also probable that any step taken in this direction by a proletarian state will be seen by conservatives and anarchists as a step backward, just as today it is said mockingly to those who once waxed indignant over legal abortion and the socialization of children that Soviet Russia is 'going backward' as it abolishes legal abortion and endeavors to reconstruct normal family life. Finally, it is certain that the superstitions, in the true sense of the term (degenerate religions, blind faith, sentimental residues of mysticisms whose objects and methods have passed into oblivion, etc.), which the same proletarian country is rooting out were poisoned foods, but foods offered (often with the deliberate intent to enslave) to satisfy real hungers. However, it is not enough to take away from an invalid the food which is killing him; you have to follow it up with healthful nourishment. At present, it is clear that scientific knowledge does not suffice to satisfy the hunger to know; nor is it enough, in order to cultivate a man, to give him an intellectual education, plus an artistic education, plus a physical education, plus a political education. And the need for a more real education and a more real culture intended for the individual himself and not just for his external appearances will summon up men capable of the job: for civilization, it will be a matter of life or death.

But, I repeat, this is utopian thinking. The fact is that in the near future, history being irreversible, two avenues are opening: fascism and the proletarian revolution. The first leads with certainty to the crushing of the individual, to blind mysticisms, and to the abasement of intellectual research, which will be limited to the invention of new means (material and other) of destruction. The second leads perhaps to a better society in which human consciousness will no longer be mechanized by mere verbal knowledge and scientism any more than it is lulled asleep by promises of paradise or terrorized by threats of hell. Sure to lose in the first case, I'm betting on the 'perhaps.' I say 'perhaps' in order to say the least. My heart would like to say 'surely,' but today I'm keeping it silent.

2. THREE DRAFTS OF AN OUTLINE
OF THE WORK

First Sheet

APPEAL

HISTORICAL BACKGROUND

PROVOCATIONS

    I. *The vision of the Absurd*
      int. of self: *Rev. of Laughter*
      int. of the world: *Pataphysics*
      metaph. exp.: CCl_4[1]

    II. *The painful Scandal*

REVOLT, first act of self-denial

THE MOMENT OF IRONY

APPEAL

That one must awaken immediately
On Metaphysics as supreme science

METAPHYSICAL INTUITION IN HISTORY

1. Being and not-being, correlative
Substitutes for thought, instruments of social oppression
Revolution is Awakening.

2. The phenomenon of religion as awakening and sleep

PROVOCATIONS TO SELF-DENIAL

By which man is provoked to think: the *Intolerable*

I. The vision of the Absurd
The Revelation of Laughter or *The absurd evidence of the
intuited self*
Reflection daughter of scandal
Denial of self and human alchemy: separate, then reunite
what was separated, but without sliding back into
original sleep
Pataphysics or *The absurd evidence of the intuition of the world*
CCl_4 or The . . .
The vision of the Abs. as model of metaphysical
experiment CCl_4

II. The painful Scandal: *Suffering*. Panalgia

III. *Revolt*, first act of self-denial
The Moment of Irony. Depict.
It's actually a limit-state: passage from rebel to revolutionary; goes beyond it:
1) as an act
2) as death
3) temptation-summonses. Same ones, in a new light
(cf. alchemy)

APPEAL TO CONSCIOUSNESS

that one must awaken immediately
On Metaphysics as supreme science

METAPHYSICAL INTUITION IN HISTORY

Thought is informed in its own tomb
Substitutes for thought, instruments of slumber and social
    oppression
Revolution is Awakening.
The phenomenon of religion as awakening and sleep:
    Revelation and Theologies
Science as awakening and sleep:
    Thought and Techniques
Art as awakening and sleep:
    Poetry and (Fine Arts)
Individual manifestations

PROVOCATIONS TO SELF-DENIAL.

    I. *The vision of the Absurd*. – *The Revelation of Laughter* or the
    absurd evidence of the intuited self
        Reflection daughter of Scandal
        Denial of self and human alchemy:
            Separate, then . . . but without . . .
        Pataphysics or the abs. ev. of the intuition of the world
       . . . .

    II. *Suffering*. – The scandal experienced, the painful absurd
        Panalgia
        Double-edged suffering. A lack. Awareness of a lack

REVOLT

Awakening, first act of self-denial
Double edge
From Revolt to Revolution

THE MOMENT OF IRONY

Second-order provocations

THE FUNDAMENTAL FACT

the act of consciousness and its double face: sleeping, waking
the mechanisms (pianist, writing, etc.)
habit, custom
Social mechanism, ultimately, must be overcome just as the
corporal mechanism is already.

I

It will always be most beneficial (didactically) to try as best one can
to set out all forms of reasoning as vicious circles: thus, the mind is
put on notice to extricate itself, and to do so *thinking* is necessary.

2 views on science:

1) vulgo – (pragmatism's universal hidden agenda): means by
which not to think (thanks to logical ordering).

2) Pataphysics: provocations to think (thanks to vicious circu-
larity).

II

Pataphysics. – Jarry's definition (nonpejorative). Humor applied to
exact sciences.

To know X = to know $(-X)$ only way to know the irreducible.

Pataphysics is the reverse of physics.

I can balance a Joe Blow against the rest of the universe.

There is no knowledge of the irreducible but through the identi-
fication of self with all – (because: irreducible to *what*? Let's say:
irreducible to X; it's enough to make X = all in order that . . . etc.)
Whence two fundamental axioms: 1) identity of opposites. 2) progress of consciousness.

Value of pataphysical sophisms.

The pataphysical sophism is an apparent sophism which envelops
an apparent truth which envelops an apparent sophism which envelops an apparent truth, and so on ad infinitum.

Formal logic of Pataphysics – On pataphysical reasoning – It progresses through pataphysical sophisms going from the arbitrary,
from pure fantasy, to necessity, to absolute rigor; each of these terms
containing the other in its turn, and each expressing one aspect at a
time of the same reality: the identity of the two terms.

Contents of Pataphysics: 'the irreducible' (Meyerson[2]); now, the irreducible is such only with regard to an attempt at synthesis in actu-

ality: the only attempt at synthesis in actuality that I can know is that of my consciousness. Thus pataphysics shifts knowledge from some abstract, universal comprehension to a particular state of consciousness, to a particular capability for synthesis – that is, to a particular stage in a mind's assimilation of the world (one must interpret the meaning thus: irreducible to a real synthesis in actuality, not merely to the abstract synthesis of Science, oh great Meyerson).

Pataphysics shall study thus the role of coloration, of *per-fection*, apparently of whim, of man's fancy in the area of knowledge.

Extensively in action – Cf. Tao.

And in art

in industry, arts and crafts, bureaucracy, government, etc.

Pataphysical theory of light – In which traditional optics will enter in as a particular incidence of pataphysical optics.

Social Pataphysics –

[blank][3]

III

[This text stands as an annex to the paragraph titled 'Formal logic of Pataphysics,' pp. 31–32 of *You've Always Been Wrong*.][4]

Pataphysical arguments do not necessarily set up systems designed to demonstrate the truth of this or that proposition. They generally develop as *vicious circles* and bring the human spirit to a limit-state of stupor and scandal.

In this line of thinking we can see as pataphysical the famous old vicious circle: 'Epimenides says that all Cretans are liars; now Epimenides is a Cretan; thus he lies; thus Cretans are not liars; thus Epimenides does not lie, and all Cretans are liars . . . ' In fact, this vicious circle is more complex than it seems at first glance; in a way, it forms two loops. It should indeed be noted that 'Cretans are liars' means 'Any Cretan is a liar.' The falsity of this proposition necessarily implies (by virtue of the 'principle of oppositions') the truth of the proposition 'Some Cretan is not a liar' (or 'All Cretans are not liars'), but not the truth of 'No Cretan is a liar' (or 'All Cretans are non-liars'). The vicious circle appears thus in two indefinite dichotomous series:

Epimenides says that all Cretans are liars,
Now, Epimenides is a Cretan. Thus he lies.
Thus some Cretan is not a liar.
Thus:

I. Either Epimenides is a liar: thus, some Cretan is not a liar; thus:

   1. Epimenides is a liar: thus, some Cretan is not a liar; thus:

    {   a) Epimenides is a liar . . . etc.
       b) Epimenides is not a liar . . . etc.

   2. Epimenides is not a liar: thus all Cretans are liars; thus Epimenides is a liar. Thus some Cretan is not a liar; thus:

    {   a) Epimenides is a liar . . . etc.
       b) Epimenides is not a liar . . . etc.

II. Or Epimenides is not a liar: thus all Cretans are liars; thus: Epimenides is a liar; thus: some Cretan is not a liar; thus:

   1. Epimenides is a liar . . . etc.

   2. Epimenides is not a liar . . . etc.

[In the margin of this text we read:][5]
It would be possible to escape the vicious circle by eliminating the second hypothesis; indeed, if 'Some Cretan is not a liar,' Ep., who says 'Any Cretan is a liar,' lies. Ep. is a liar, but not all Cretans are. But formal logic does not allow us to rule out this second hypothesis: for one can do so only by challenging the meaning, the content of the propositions; the very notion 'liar' itself has to be thought out.

Translator's Introduction

1. Jarry defines Pataphysics as 'the science of imaginary solutions'; see Alfred Jarry, *Gestes et opinions du docteur Faustroll, pataphysicien*, in *Œuvres complètes*, vol.1 (Paris: Pléiade, 1972), 668–70. See also Roger Shattuck, 'What is "Pataphysics?," ' in *The Innocent Eye* (New York: Farrar Straus Giroux, 1984), 102–6.

2. 'Le souvenir déterminant,' in René Daumal, *Les Pouvoirs de la Parole* (Paris: Gallimard, 1972), 112.

3. Daumal himself used the term 'dharma' to qualify his calling; see *Les Pouvoirs*, 85.

4. Daumal's theory of poetics, translatable as 'Clavicles (or "Little Keys") to a Poetic Great Game'; see René Daumal, *L'Evidence Absurde* (Paris: Gallimard, 1972), 57–81.

5. David Loy, *Nonduality: A Study in Comparative Philosophy* (New Haven: Yale University Press, 1988), 249.

6. See André Breton, *Oeuvres complètes*, vol.1 (Paris: Gallimard, 1988), 979–86.

7. *L'Evidence Absurde*, 150–51.

8. *L'Evidence Absurde*, 161.

9. See 'Lettre ouverte à André Breton,' in *L'Evidence Absurde*, 153–59.

10. Cf. the epigraph to Jack Daumal's introduction, which is taken from the same letter to Breton.

11. Cf. Breton's formula, which begins with 'tout porte à croire' ('everything leads us to believe').

12. In his essay 'Politique de René Daumal,' published in *René Daumal, Dossiers* (Paris: L'Age d'Homme, 1993), Pascal Sigoda convincingly argues the case that Daumal eschewed the right and espoused the left – even in his later years.

13. In fact, this edition retains the section titles which Jack Daumal added to the original manuscript in order to delineate 'the text's natural divisions into sections.' These are, in the order of their appearance in this text: 'Spiritual Death,' 'Truisms,' 'The Absolute . . . ,' 'The Word

"God," ' 'India and Tibet,' 'So! You Want to Think Freely!,' 'The Sages of India,' 'Christ on the Mount of Olives,' 'Dogmaclastic Institutes,' 'Why Write a Book?,' and 'Metaphysics.' The first two of these sections, 'Spiritual Death' and 'Truisms,' have been grouped together for the present edition in a chapter with the title 'An Appeal to Consciousness,' taken from the first heading of the 'Third Sheet' of the 'Three Drafts of an Outline' in Appendix 2.

14. Jarry, *Œuvres complètes*, 668.

15. In *Les Pouvoirs*, 136.

Introduction

1. This epigraph is taken from René Daumal's now-famous 'Open letter to André Breton concerning relations between Surrealism and the *Grand Jeu*,' first published in *Le Grand Jeu* (no.3), autumn 1930 (although Jack Daumal gives the date as 1929), 76–83. – TV

2. Josef Sima, an artist and member of the *Grand Jeu* group. – TV

3. Despite the 'aggressive intentions' which Marc Thivolet (understandably) insists on proclaiming in his introductory article 'concerning those who are ready to decide the *Grand Jeu*'s fate in the name of literary history; that is to say, to bury it under piles of praise and exegesis.' – JD

4. Alexandre de Salzmann, who introduced Daumal to the teachings of Gurdjieff in 1930. – TV

5. In fact, the preface was written in 1935. In the same year, *Le Contre-Ciel* (*The Counter-Sky*) was honored by a literary prize: the Prix Jacques Doucet. – TV

6. The essay in question, which Daumal wrote in 1929, is 'Clavicules d'un grand jeu poétique' ('Clavicles to a poetic great game' – with 'clavicles' in the sense of 'small keys'); it was also published in *L'Evidence Absurde*. – TV

7. Immediately after the word 'follow,' Jack Daumal leaves an ellipsis where René Daumal had written 'and which are older' – that is, older than the essay 'Clavicles.' – TV

8. Names of *Grand Jeu* collaborators. – TV

9. The capitalized 'Traditions' is no doubt meant to differentiate the metaphysical Tradition spoken of by esotericists and treated, for example, in Aldous Huxley's *The Perennial Philosophy* (1944) from culture based in tradition. – TV

10. The capitalized 'Teaching' refers to the practices of the Gurdjieff groups active in France at the time. – TV

You've Always Been Wrong

1. In the margin: 'no.' – JD

    That is to say: René Daumal added the comment 'no' in the margin some years after writing the manuscript. This is the first of Daumal's marginal notes mentioned by Jack Daumal in the brief section appended at the end of his introduction. – TV

2. In the margin: 'dialectical!' – JD

3. I wish to emphasize with this proviso the rarity of the occurrence. – RD

4. '*Prima materia*' is the traditional alchemical term denoting nature in its primordial state before differentiation. Daumal writes 'pierre brute'; I feel 'raw stone,' although in keeping with the prosaic side of Daumal's discursive register, may be misleading. Conversely, 'Great Work' (for Daumal's 'Grand Oeuvre') is often seen in writings on alchemy in place of 'magnum opus.' – TV

5. With a few minor changes, a portion of the preceding section ('The Revelation of Laughter'), from its beginning up to the words 'a forward dash which denies the goal,' was published in 1929 in the journal *Bifur* and placed after the present section ('Pataphysics') whose first few lines were deleted up to 'personified by Faustroll'; together they were titled 'Pataphysics and the Revelation of Laughter.'

    A few pages were included in *Chaque fois que l'aube paraît* with this same title; but they were clearly titled in the author's own handwriting: 'On Pataphysical Laughter; that it threatens awakening.' In point of fact, these pages appear to be a draft of the text published in this volume and also therefore of the article published in *Bifur*. – JD

    René Daumal's *Chaque fois que l'aube paraît* (Each Time the Dawn Appears), subtitled 'Essais et Notes, I,' was published by Gallimard in 1953.

    The essay also appears, two years after the publication date of the Mercure de France edition of *Tu t'es toujours trompé*, under the title 'La Pataphysique et la Révélation du Rire' in the 1972 Gallimard re-edition of Daumal's 'Essays and Notes' titled *L'Evidence Absurde*. In the Gallimard volume, the essay's order follows that of the *Bifur* text. A translation of this version is included in René Daumal, *The Powers of the Word*, trans. Mark Polizzotti (San Francisco: City Lights, 1991), 15–22, under the title 'Pataphysics and the Revelation of Laughter.' – TV

6. Reference to a character in Book 4 of Jarry's *Exploits and Opinions of Doctor Faustroll, Pataphysician*. – TV

7. For 'Joe Blow,' the original French is *tête de pipe*. 'Pipe bowl,' a more literal translation, is not adequate to convey its resonance with the expression *par tête de pipe*, which means colloquially 'per person,' that is, 'per individual.' Daumal's rather humorous use of *tête de pipe*, while evoking individuality, is meant to connote the anonymous individual in the crowd, 'John Q. Public,' and, by extension, whatever is designated or set off as a discrete unit. 'Joe Blow' seems best suited to suggest the humorous overtones of *tête de pipe*. – TV

8. This passage is particularly helpful for understanding the legend of Ho and Mo in *Mount Analogue*. – TV

9. We include at the end of this volume (Documents, 3) a few pages found in René Daumal's manuscripts which refer either to the present section ('Pataphysics') in its entirety or to certain of its passages. – JD

    Jack Daumal's note refers to 'Diverse Notes on Pataphysics,' to be found in Appendix 3 in the present edition. – TV

10. Isidore Ducasse, more usually known by the pen name Lautréamont, author of *Les Chants de Maldoror* mentioned below. – TV

11. Because algebra is prematurely taught in secondary schools, many a student who waltzes through third-degree equations finds himself incapable of solving logically a quite simple arithmetic problem; in the same situation, a primary pupil will often prove to be more capable. – RD

12. *Going to the limit*: an essential process in metaphysical reflection; summarily mentioned here, it will be studied later in a more precise and systematic fashion. We will justify it as being both the source of all metaphysical notions and the basis of all knowledge. – RD

    In an essay on Emile Meyerson intended for the never-published fourth number of *Le Grand Jeu*, Daumal states: 'What distinguishes metaphysical thought is that it continually goes to the limit, to use the mathematical term.' In a footnote to the word 'limit,' he adds: 'This should not be interpreted as the expectation of a future state, but rather a way of seeing things in their absolute value, sub specie æternitatis.' See Daumal, *L'Evidence Absurde*, 204. – TV

13. Today, the Vietnamese. – TV

14. The blanks which follow reproduce those in the manuscript which Daumal intended to fill with citations probably to be taken from the *Chandogya Upanishad*. – JD

15. A blank in the manuscript. – JD

16. A blank in the manuscript. – JD

17. The issue of castes and the caste system, only briefly touched upon here, was later treated in René Daumal's writings in two texts which we mention without further ado so as to avoid any possible misunderstanding: 'Les Limites du langage philosophique' (1935) and 'Pour approcher l'art poétique hindou' (1941), both published in *Chaque fois que l'aube paraît*. – JD

Both of these essays were later republished by Gallimard. The second is included in René Daumal's *Bharata* (Paris: Gallimard, 1970), a collection concentrating on Daumal's writings on matters pertaining to Indian aesthetics. Both are included in *Les Pouvoirs de la Parole* (1972), the second volume of Daumal's 'essays and notes.'

In English, 'Les limites . . .' is published as 'The Limits of Philosophical Language' in Mark Polizzotti's edition and translation of Daumal's essays, *The Powers of the Word*; 'Pour approcher . . .' is published as 'To Approach the Hindu Poetic Art' in Louise Landes Levi's edition and translation of Daumal's *Bharata* under the title *Rasa* (New York: New Directions, 1982). – TV

18. This paragraph, brackets included, is Jack Daumal's commentary as it is inserted into the body of the text. – TV

19. The seven sentences contained between this note and the next are highlighted in the margin with emphatic question marks which seem to indicate that René no longer 'agreed' with this passage when re-reading long after he wrote it. – JD

In the original text, the footnotes are the letters 'a' and 'b' in superscript. The placement of this note and the next in our text correspond accordingly to their placement in the original. – TV

20. See preceding note. – TV

21. In the margin next to this sentence: 'What gall!' – JD

22. Cf. Alexandra David-Neel, *Mystiques et magiciens du Thibet. Initiations lamaïques.* – RD

   This work was originally published in Paris in 1929 by Plon. In English translation, it is *Magic and Mystery in Tibet*, trans. A. D'Arsonval (New York: Dover, 1971). – TV

23. In the margin: 'Poor me!' – JD

24. In the margin, even with the name 'Plekhanov,' René had written 'Oh! Plekhanov' in pencil and drawn below it the Bolshevik emblem of the hammer and sickle topped by a five-pointed star. – JD

   Georgi Valentinovich Plekhanov (1856–1918), considered the founder of Russian Marxism, at first sided with Lenin, then became a Menshevik; he fled Russia after the autumn 1917 Bolshevik takeover. – TV

25. Hegel, *Philosophy of Nature* (on the Bhagavad-Gita). – RD

26. In a letter written to Carlo Suarès in the spring of 1932, Daumal will refer to 'certain articles of the statutes of the Theosophical Society in India, which singularly tie that organization to the Intelligence Service'; see René Daumal, *Correspondance, 1929–1932* (Paris: Gallimard, 1993), 282. – TV

27. This remark on René Guénon is tagged in the margin with a large question mark, which is in no way surprising . . . – JD

   Presumably, René Daumal's question mark is not 'surprising,' because of Guénon's reputation as a traditionalist reactionary. – TV

28. René Guénon, *L'Homme et son devenir selon le Védanta*; *Le Roi du monde*; *Autorité spirituelle et pouvoir temporel*, etc. – RD

   These three volumes were published respectively in 1925, 1927, and 1929. Of the three, two have appeared in English translation: *Man and His Becoming According to the Vedanta* (London: Luzac, 1945), and *The Lord of the World* (Ellingstring, England: Coombe Springs Press, 1983). – TV

29. A Christian devotional book traditionally ascribed to Thomas à Kempis, a German monk said to have written it around 1425. – TV

30. Again, in the margin, a large question mark, with the written comment: 'but . . . (no proletariat) . . . Ramakrishna, Vivekananda.' – JD

31. According to Jack Daumal's comments in the 'Documents' section of the original Mercure de France edition of *Tu t'es toujours trompé*, a file bearing the title 'Affaire Dieu' (God Affair) was found among René Daumal's papers after his death. The file contained the manuscript and two copies of 'Poem to God and Man' together with a number of letters he had received from various sources giving documentary evidence of the events, circumstances, and attitudes which prevented the poem from being published until its insertion in *Tu t'es toujours trompé* in 1970.

In the spring of 1932, Daumal was retained by Lise Deharme, who was launching a new literary review, *Le Phare de Neuilly* (*The Neuilly Beacon*). Despite the objections voiced by his friend and collaborator André Rolland de Renéville in a letter of 21 May 1932 to Daumal ('concerning the Neuilly Searchlight, allow me to insist that you *immediately* withdraw your poem from that shitbog'), Daumal allowed the poem to be published. But, fearing scandal, 'Lady Deharme' (as Renéville called her) gathered up all undistributed copies of the issue and had the pages unbound so that the pages on which the poem was printed could be removed. Word of what she had done reached Henri Michaux and Antonin Artaud, both of whom consequently refused to collaborate on the review. Most importantly, Jean Paulhan, then editor-in-chief of the prestigious *Nouvelle Revue Française*, also got wind of the affair and reacted by publishing in the monthly feature 'Review of Reviews' a short paragraph stating that the *Phare de Neuilly* had published in its first issue a beautiful poem by Daumal; immediately following the statement was the poem's first verse.

Next in line for the poem was the *Cahiers du Sud*, whose editor, Jean Ballard, refused it in December 1933, this time not for fear of scandal but because it was against the review's policy to publish anything having to do with God: 'We don't talk about God at the *Cahiers*, we ignore him.'

Again, in 1934, even though it was championed by Franz Hellens, who wanted it for a collection of poetry he would publish titled *Au disque vert*, it was turned down for reasons almost identical to those of Lise Deharme. A year later, Hellens wrote to Daumal, saying he would like to try to get it published in *Ecrits du Nord*, a new review based in Brussels. But for whatever reasons the manuscript did not arrive in time for publication, and by October 1935 *Ecrits du Nord* was defunct. – TV

32. The 'Poem to God and Man' is in effect a parenthesis in the text of the essay; 'moreover' simply picks up where the preceding sentence of the text left off. – TV

33. Gérard de Nerval, *Les Chimères* – RD

   Les Chimères is a collection of twelve sonnets composed between 1843 and 1854; the narrator of each one, like the Christ of the sonnet Daumal quotes, is a solitary being confronting silence and nothingness.

   Daumal professed a strong affinity for Nerval in his 1930 essay, 'Nerval le Nyctalope,' which he wrote for number three of *Le Grand Jeu*. In it, he contended that, rather than fiction or poetry, Nerval's writing was in fact a chronicle of lived experience very similar to his own: 'Nerval went there . . . he describes to me what I saw there, often even what I experienced there.' – TV

34. The practice of locking up 'criminals' (that is, those who are reputed as such by society) was invented by the Holy Inquisition. It was supposed to 'bring back stray sheep to the Lord.' What's it supposed to do today? – RD

35. Emphatically written in the margin: 'no way!' – JD

36. In the margin: 'Oh! dia   lectics!' – JD

37. In the margin: 'O dialectics!' – JD

38. In the margin: '(yes but.)' – JD

39. The passage encompassed between this note and the next one is marked in the margin by a large question mark. – JD

40. See preceding note. – TV

41. I use the forms 'idealist' and 'materialist' to convey 'premises of idealists' and 'conclusions of materialists,' rather than 'idealistic premises' and 'materialistic conclusions.' This same usage continues in following paragraphs. – TV

42. Although the German philosopher Bruno Bauer (1809–82) interpreted Hegel's philosophy as antithetical to Christianity, he was nonetheless a Hegelian seen by Marx as more interested in theory than in practice. – TV

43. In the margin: small question mark. – JD
44. In the margin next to the two preceding subordinate clauses: a question mark. – JD

    Pierre-Auguste Villiers de l'Isle-Adam (1838–89), French novelist and dramatist often classified as a symbolist, wrote a number of short stories in the fantastic genre. – TV
45. Cf. the 'Postface to the Second Edition' of *Capital*, written by Marx in London, 24 January 1973. – TV
46. In the margin next to this sentence and the following: a question mark. – JD

    Félix Alexandre Le Dantec (1869–1917) defended Lamarck's theories of transformation. – TV
47. Cf. Daumal's subtitle to his *Mount Analogue*: 'A Novel of Symbolically Authentic Non-Euclidean Adventures in Mountain Climbing.' – TV
48. This is a literal rendition of what seems to be an unintentionally elliptical sentence, perhaps a lapse of attention on Daumal's part. If I were to add my interpretation to the translation, it would read: 'It is of the essence of thought to think all things as determined, and to think the thinker's language as equal to any other object.' – TV
49. In the margin next to this and the next sentence: 'laugh or cry?' – JD
50. Presumably an allusion to the First World War. – TV
51. In the margin: 'Dialec . . . what?' – JD
52. Cf. the first few pages of 'Spiritual Death.' – TV
53. From this point to the end of the sentence, in the margin: 'Reckless!' – JD
54. The original French text gives 'Haeck.' Daumal is clearly referring to Ernst Heinrich Haeckel (1834–1919), a German biologist and philosopher whose monistic theory of recapitulation – which sees the development of an embryo as mirroring the evolutionary development of the species – is commonly expressed as 'ontogeny recapitulates phylogeny.' – TV

Appendixes

1. Carbon tetrachloride (see, in translator's introduction, the brief discussion of Daumal's youthful 'experiments'). – TV
2. In a polemical essay written for number four of *Le Grand Jeu* (which

was never published), Daumal attacked Emile Meyerson (1859–1933), a French philosopher and scientist of Polish origin, for having pushed aside the inexplicable aspects of nature as 'irreducible.' The essay was later published in *L'Evidence Absurde*, 199–208. – TV

3. JD's note. – TV

4. JD's note. – TV

5. JD's note. – TV

INDEX

Jean Paulhan
Progress in Love on the Slow Side
Translated by
Christine Moneera Laennec
and Michael Syrotinski

Benjamin Péret
Death to the Pigs, and Other
Writings
Translated by Rachel Stella
and Others

Boris Vian
Blues for a Black Cat and
Other Stories
Edited and translated by Julia Older